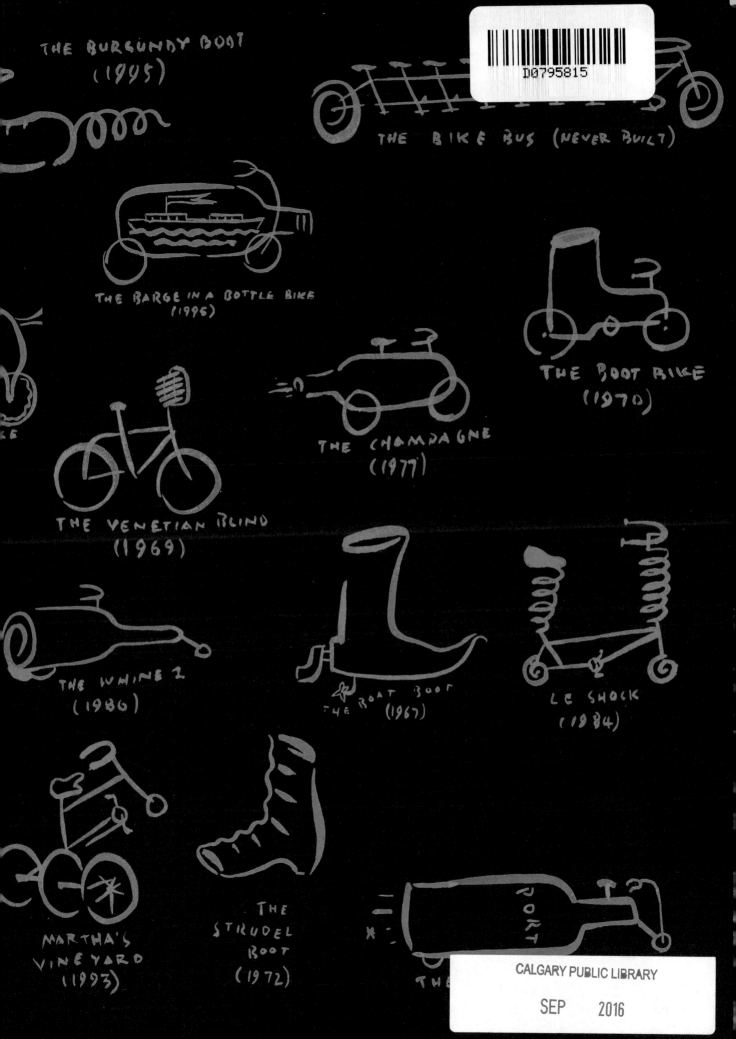

THE BURGUNDY BOOT
(1995)

THE BIKE BUS (NEVER BUILT)

THE BARGE IN A BOTTLE BIKE
(1995)

THE BOOT BIKE
(1970)

THE CHAMPAGNE
(1977)

THE VENETIAN BLIND
(1969)

THE WHINE 2
(1986)

THE BOAT BOOT (1967)

LE SHOCK
(1984)

MARTHA'S
VINEYARD
(1993)

THE
STRUDEL
BOOT
(1972)

THE

Butterfield &Robinson

Butterfield & Robinson Inc.
70 Bond Street, 3rd Floor
Toronto, Ontario
M5B 1X3

Distributed in Canada by
House of Anansi Press through:

Distributed in the United States by
House of Anansi Press through:

University of Toronto Press
5201 Dufferin Street
Toronto, ON M3H 5T8
Toll free tel. 1-800-565-9523

Publishers Group West
1700 Fourth Street
Berkeley, CA 94710
Toll free tel. 1-800-788-3123

20 19 18 17 16 1 2 3 4 5

Library and Archives Canada Cataloguing in Publication
Scott, Charlie, 1971–, author
Slowing down to see the world: 50 years of biking and walking with Butterfield & Robinson / Charlie Scott.

ISBN: 978-1-4870-0071-4 (paperback).

1. Butterfield & Robinson – History. 2. Travel agents – Canada –

History. I. Title.

G154.S36 2016   910   C2015-904788-9
C2015-904789-7

Library of Congress Control Number: 2015954897

Author: Charlie Scott
Cover design: Viva & Co.
Text design and typesetting: Viva & Co.
Editor: Rosemary Shipton

We acknowledge for their financial support of our publishing program the Canada Council for the Arts, the Ontario Arts Council, and the Government of Canada through the Canada Book Fund.

Printed and bound in Canada

This paper has been certified to meet the environmental and social standards of the Forest Stewardship Council® (FSC®) and comes from well-managed forests and other responsible sources.

1

1952
-
1965

Sprouts & Sparks

TERAR DUM PROSIM

A lot can happen over lunch. On a drizzly autumn day in 1957 George Butterfield and Sidney Robinson, eighteen and nineteen, respectively, decided to make the most of the occasion. Young men on a mission, they selected a restaurant that would reflect their seriousness and maturity – a fancy and impressive establishment. They reserved a table at The Stoodleigh, a long-standing but no-longer-there restaurant in downtown Toronto. A *ye olde* throwback, it had wood-panelled walls, a stone fireplace, Windsor chairs, and brass chandeliers – the sort of place you'd feel odd *not* ordering the prime rib roast with Yorkshire pudding.

Sitting at a white-linen-draped table in their jackets and ties, trying not to fidget with the heavy cutlery, George and Sidney waited for their guest to arrive. His name was Dick Gibb, a high school geography teacher at St. Andrew's College in Aurora and co-owner of Gibb-Macfarlane, a Canadian student travel company. They had invited Dick to lunch so they could hit him up for a job.

The road that led to that meeting began five years before when George and Sidney arrived at Ridley College, a prestigious boys'

"I thought she was about the coolest girl on the planet"

boarding school in St. Catharines. "Day one, he was the first person I met," recalls George. Their beds were a foot apart in the dorm, and they quickly became best friends, often talking late into the night about the finer points of life – or more specifically, girls. George's parents lived in Bermuda, so when the mid-term break rolled around, Sidney invited him to stay with his family in Toronto. Big brother to two younger sisters, Sidney was especially keen for George to meet the older one, Martha, a sparky twelve-year-old. "I thought she was about the coolest girl on the planet," says Sidney, "yet George had very little interest in her."

As they neared the end of grade 13, the final year of high school in Ontario, George and Sidney cooked up the idea of a summer trip to Europe to celebrate their graduation. They would backpack around

the Continent, exploring and experiencing newfound freedom on their own – or so they hoped. The boys pitched the plan to their parents, but George's father and Sidney's mother (the sergeants in each household) quickly deflated the dream on the grounds that the boys were too young, couldn't speak most European languages, and would only get into trouble. After many rounds of discussion they agreed on a compromise: George and Sidney would travel to Europe on a chaperoned group trip with Gibb-Macfarlane Student Tours.

For several years Dick Gibb and his friend and business partner, Stan Macfarlane (a French teacher at St. Andrew's College), had been spending their summers leading forty to fifty students on five-week journeys through Europe. Air travel was still a luxury (or at least a rarity), so they went by ship between Montreal and London. From there the itineraries meandered through Germany, Switzerland, Italy, and France before looping back to Great Britain.

As stated in their simple brochure, the trips had the twofold aim of providing a "relaxing and enjoyable" holiday and delivering an "education in international living, taught by the best teacher of all, personal experience." They emphasized self-reliance and freedom of choice whenever possible, building into the journey some days of urban exploring and rural rambling as well as days of doing nothing by the sea. They stayed in basic hotels and guest houses, stopped at village cafés, ate at trattorias, drank at weinstubes, and included visits to classic monuments and sights such as the Pantheon in Rome and the Louvre in Paris. Travel was mostly by train, but the students hiked in the Alps and spent a week bicycling in southern Germany and Switzerland – invariably a highlight of the summer. The Gibb-Macfarlane trips were a distillation of the European good life and an evolution of the Grand Tour.

For George and Sidney, the experience of travelling through Europe for the first time in the summer of 1957 was mind blowing. From their backgrounds in small island Bermuda and provincial Toronto, they had suddenly landed in a continent that was bursting with history and culture, buzzing with street life, and jammed with gastronomic delight and scenic beauty. As soon as they arrived back in Canada they set their sights on returning to Europe the following summer. But how?

During the trip, George and Sidney had noticed that the helpers Gibb-Macfarlane hired to schlep bags and keep the students out of trouble were retired teachers – well-meaning people who were challenged to fix flat tires and quite unable to race the luggage up four flights of stairs. They sensed an opportunity. So, as George recalls, "we called up Dick Gibb and invited him to lunch at The Stoodleigh."

At the appointed hour, Dick greeted the boys in his congenial and particular way of speaking – a Boston Brahmin-like drawl that could smoothly pull a vowel the full length of a word. Sidney wasted little time getting to business. "Here's the thing," he began over the first course, and outlined the reasons Gibb-Macfarlane should hire them for the following summer. "We sold him on the fact that we had charm, chutzpah, and all the rest," says George. Dick found the proposal compelling and agreed to bring the dynamic young duo along for the next season.

But Sidney wasn't quite done. He insisted they should be paid. As George remembers, "Dick explained that the schoolteachers didn't get paid because they got a free summer in Europe, but Sidney said that wasn't good enough for them." By the time the meal was done, George and Sidney had been hired for $500 each to be the Gibb-Macfarlane baggage boys for the next trip.

"We sold him on the fact that we had charm, chutzpah, and all the rest"

For the following four summers, from 1958 to 1961, George and Sidney returned to Europe and worked as right- and left-hand men to Dick and Stan. Only a couple of years older than most of the students on the trip, they quickly proved their worth as reliable, mature, and fun additions to the mix. Sidney, who had taken art history courses during his years at the University of Toronto, delivered guided tours as the students visited the great cities, galleries, and museums of Europe. At the time, most of the official tour guides were Second World War veterans with weak skills in English and little knowledge of history and art. "I'd be listening and saying to the girl standing next to me in the room, 'Well, you know, what he's saying isn't quite right – this is Baroque, not Rococo,'" remembers Sidney. "Pretty soon I noticed three-quarters of the group were listening to me and not the guide." Following in Stan's footsteps, the smart and scholarly Sidney became Gibb-Macfarlane's rising cultural emissary.

EUBLE FRICERO
1 rue Fricéro - 1er Etage
A VENDRE
RCHÉ
AU PETIT MARCHÉ
MARCHAND
DROGUER
ommes
1.80
4.50

....

RIGHT
*George, Dick, and
a van in seemingly
fine repair*

FAR RIGHT
Stan Macfarlane

The Little Goat Farmer

It would have been weird if George hadn't developed a taste for business. His father, Dudley Butterfield, and his grandfather, Harry St. George Butterfield, were both entrepreneurs – their names alone worth a franchise. Harry got things rolling in 1923 when he inked a deal to import biscuits from the United Kingdom to Bermuda, a venture that soon became Butterfield & Company. Dudley assumed the helm a few decades later and grew the food-importing business substantially while simultaneously running nearly a dozen other ventures – from office equipment to building materials, accounting to insurance, real estate to cement, and even a flower shop.

It wasn't a huge surprise to Dudley when nine-year-old George announced over dinner one evening that he was ready to start a business of his own. He wanted to be a goat farmer. Dudley wasn't immediately sold on the idea and laughed it off. But young George was serious and wouldn't let it go. "I kept bugging him and bugging him,

George, meanwhile, was developing a keen interest in the business side of things, shadowing Dick and learning from him how to organize and operate a trip. His education went beyond numbers and logistics. Described by one of his former students as a cross between Sean Connery and Ernest Hemingway, Dick was a *bon vivant*, a man's man, a true character. "He had the capacity for a whole lot of laughs," remembers George. "I picked up a lot of that, whatever it was, the fun side of business." Perhaps more important than anything else, he taught George how to slow down.

One of the biggest chores of moving fifty students around Europe was shuttling their luggage from place to place. Gibb-Macfarlane rented a van to do the job, and some of the time it was Dick and George's responsibility to drive the bags while Stan and Sidney took the students on the train. On one particularly hot August day, Dick and George slowly made their way from Florence to Rome in a van stuffed with dozens of hard-sided suitcases.

The heat became unbearable once they left the Tuscan hills behind and approached the coast. When they rolled into the picturesque town of Talamone, Dick pulled the van to the side of the melting asphalt. "I think you better call Stan right now and tell him we have

driving him crazy," says George, "until finally he said 'Okay' and arranged for me to buy a goat from a nearby farmer."

The new asset was tied to a stake behind the garage at the family home on Point Shares Road in Bermuda. At first George relished the responsibility of feeding and caring for the goat, but after a few days of waking early to clean up the mess the animal invariably made on the lawn, he was weary of the process. "The farmer came over and took the goat back," recalls George, "and that was the end of that."

It may have been the end of George's foray into farming, but it certainly wasn't the end of his enthusiasm for business. Though he was raised with undeniable privilege, the family work ethic spurred an entrepreneurial zeal that kept George sharp and determined to create something from nothing.

trouble with the differential," he said, speaking slowly and deliberately so George would grasp the meaning of this fabricated story. "Tell the kids we're sorry, but the bags won't be there until one or two in the morning." Then, turning to George he chuckled: "You and I have got to have a swim in the ocean and a nice dinner."

"On my own I would never have done that," says George. But he wasn't on his own. That day he learned perhaps his most important lesson from Dick – to temper hard work with lightness and laughter, and on extremely hot days, a swim and some grappa. To go slow to see the world...

It's hard to exaggerate what a great experience the Gibb-Macfarlane tours became for George and Sidney. While most of their friends were planting trees in northern Ontario or working at resort hotels in the Canadian Rockies to earn $300 to $400 over the summer, they were having a blast in Europe. As Sidney puts it, "By then we were making three or four times that plus all the wine, all the travel, all the art you could imagine."

As much as the summers in Europe were fun, they couldn't go on forever. By the fall of 1962, having completed their undergraduate degrees, both George and Sidney were feeling the weight of parental expectations. It was time to get serious and set travel aside. George enrolled at Osgoode Hall Law School in Toronto while Sidney taught philosophy at the University of Toronto and completed a master's degree (two years later he too was studying law). Though George had always been a good student, he found law school a slog. Sure, it was a responsible, legitimate path, but not one that fed his spirit.

The extracurricular front was far more vibrant. Martha Robinson was back in Toronto from Paris, where she'd spent a third year abroad, and she and George began to spend more and more time together. For years now George had been a regular guest at the Robinson house, and the young ones had often gone to movies and other outings together. "But then," remembers Martha, "George was

....
LEFT
*Beaming young
Butterfields*

RIGHT
*Sidney, his sister
Mary, and George
lunch with a friend*

BELOW
*Martha scooting
through
Switzerland*

NEXT
*Ever-inviting
Amalfi Coast*

at Osgoode and asked me to the big law school dance weeks ahead! So I was thinking, 'What's going on here?'" She went to the dance.

Eight months later, in September 1963, George and Martha were engaged. Before long they bought a small house on Bishop Street in Toronto's Yorkville area. Sidney wasn't sure what to make of the double-barrelled news. "He knew we'd been seeing each other," says Martha, "but when I told him he turned ashen. He thought he had lost his best friend – his two best friends." If anything, the friendships were braiding them all closer together. In the spring of 1964, when George and Martha got married, she became the first true Butterfield *and* Robinson, foreshadowing by name the company to be.

With the responsibilities of the adult world inching ever closer, George, Sidney, and Martha yearned again to return to Europe. Three years had passed since George and Sidney's last summer of guiding for Gibb-Macfarlane. They missed the freedom, the fun, the food, the wine, the bicycling from town to town – the whole good life. Martha had never worked for Gibb-Macfarlane, but she had attended Neuchâtel Junior College in Switzerland for her final year of high school, studied fine art at the Institut d'art et d'archéologie at the Université de Paris (where she wrote the entrance exams in French), worked in London for an investment firm, and immersed herself in the local culture every step of the way. All three had fallen hard for Europe. By the time George finished law school in the spring of 1965, they knew they had to find a way back for the following summer. But, as before, how to do it? They had no money.

RISTORANTE FLAVIO GIOIA

"If you don't take us, we'll start our own company"

Once again George and Sidney called Dick Gibb and invited him out for lunch. This time there was less fanfare. They met at a simple diner a few steps off Yonge Street, Toronto's arterial axis and the longest street in the world. Over the years of working together, they had all become close friends, and there was a lot of warmth and mutual respect around the small formica-topped table. Before lunch even arrived, George jumped in, "Sidney, Martha, and I could really add a lot to your trips. We're young and we're starved to get back to Europe. You've got to hire us." But things had changed at Gibb-Macfarlane. A young nephew had replaced George and Sidney as the baggage boy, sales weren't as robust, and there simply wasn't any room in the company for more employees. "I can't hire you," lamented Dick, rubbing his beard as though it hurt to say no. "Well, if you don't take us, we'll start our own student tour company," Sidney argued, hoping to change his mind. But Dick Gibb did not back down.

And so Butterfield & Robinson began.

Bikers' Chic

Few things mark the passage of time as vividly as fashion. Whereas the wheel was invented but once, cyclists have continually reinvented what it means to roll in comfort and style.

YEARS	1966 - 1979	1980 - 1993

Numeric Overview
As bikes gear up, natural fibres gear down

	1966 - 1979	1980 - 1993
	3 Bike Gear Count	**94%** Cotton Content	**10** Bike Gear Count	**82%** Cotton Content

Protective headgear

Hair (bigger the better, feathered for maximum protection)

Cotton cycling cap (worn backwards sometimes, Campagnolo brand)

Upper body

Oxford cloth button down (short sleeve)

Polo shirt (Lacoste, Ralph Lauren) "collar popped," t-shirt

Lower body

Bermuda shorts (madras fabric, plaid)

Cut-off jeans, rugby shorts (Canterbury brand), tennis shorts

Feet

Boat shoes (Sperry, leather, or canvas), white knee socks

Tennis shoes (Reeboks)

Accessories du jour

RayBan Wayfarer sunglasses, terry cloth head band (wrist bands)

Mesh cycling gloves, bandana, lamb's wool seat cover

Contents of water bottle

Tap water

Chablis (white wine)

The bike

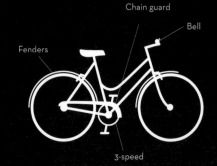

Chain guard
Bell
Fenders
3-speed

Brake cables flying all over the place
Pump
Lever gear changer
10-speed

1994 - 2000	2001 - 2011	2012 +

18 Bike Gear Count	**64%** Cotton Content	**21** Bike Gear Count	**32%** Cotton Content	**100** Bike Gear Count	**8%** Cotton Content

Plastic-covered foam bowl

Impossible to adjust but very professional hi-tech helmet

Something NASA and/or Porsche designed

Cotton t-shirt, yellow Gore-Tex windbreaker

Bright colour lycra cycling jersey (United States Postal Service, Lance Armstrong's team)

Full-body lycra cycling suit

Black Lycra shorts (first-gereration)

Branded (with anything) multi-colour lycra bike shorts

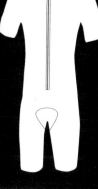

See above (Full-body lycra cycling suit)

Jogging shoes (Nike)

Cycling shoes (no laces. please)

Cycling booties

Gel seat cover, toe baskets for petals

Heart monitor, bike seat with crotch cut-out, clipless petals

GPS, face-wrapping sunglasses

Gatorade

Fiji bottled water

Diet Coke (shh, don't tell anyone), Red Bull

Grip Shift gear changer

Toe baskets for petals

18-speed

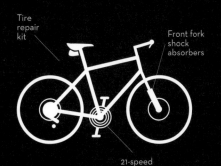

Tire repair kit

Front fork shock absorbers

21-speed

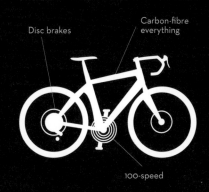

Disc brakes

Carbon-fibre everything

100-speed

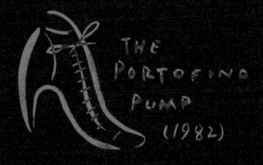

THE
PORTOFINO
PUMP
(1982)

---

*"Clothes make the man.
Naked people have little or
no influence on society."*

MARK TWAIN

2

1966
-
1979

Pioneering

European Trip for Students
July 2nd - August 29th, 1966

Butterfield & Robinson Travel
24 Bishop Street, Toronto 5, Canada Telephone WA 4-1047

Sitting on a living-room floor stuffing envelopes hardly seems like a magical start to anything, but for George, Martha, and Sidney it was an exciting first step toward their dream of returning to Europe for the summer of 1966. If Gibb-Macfarlane didn't have jobs for them, they were determined to start their own student travel company. For an investment of $1,500 they set up a makeshift office in George and Martha's home on Bishop Street in Toronto, pulled together a simple yet striking brochure, and mailed it out to several hundred homes. They'd give it a try and see if there were any takers.

"Oh, it was a lark for the summer," recalls Martha, "but still, I think back to how much work it was." Martha and Sidney whipped the words into shape, taking care to set expectations and define the Butterfield & Robinson approach: "We will not rush simply to 'do' more. We want those who come with us to develop clear impressions of places, people and events. This requires time to understand and to enjoy." George's primary job was to come up with a mailing list, which he did by taking names from their wedding roster and from membership directories of private sporting and social clubs around Toronto. "I had ten clubs," George remembers, "and I looked up the names in the phone book; the club lists didn't give the addresses. So Martha and I spent weekend after weekend after weekend just looking up the names and addresses of all the people on the lists." Martha shaped the design of the brochure and enlisted the help of David Bartholomew, a young graphic designer from the John B. Parkin architecture firm she had worked with for the previous three years. It may have been a lark, but it was going to be a good lark. As George says, "The brochure was really important. It was the one opportunity we had to distinguish ourselves as unique and creative."

Something else set Butterfield & Robinson apart. As much by chance as anything, they'd stumbled on a near perfect chemistry of character and experience. George and Sidney both knew the ropes of planning and leading trips – George's creativity and intuitive understanding of the marketing and sales side of the business matched by Sidney's natural bent for financial rigour and focus on operational detail. Martha, an art and culture aficionado, contributed a sense of flair and a powerful measure of female energy. They were young, vibrant, well educated, attractive, enthusiastic, and unfailingly fun – the refreshing entrepreneurial cocktail the travel world was waiting for. And it didn't hurt that the trio included a married couple. Referring to the chaperone culture of the time, George says: "Nobody was

"Nobody was going to send their 17-year-old daughter off with a 25-year-old bachelor. They just weren't going to do that"

going to send their seventeen-year-old daughter off with a twenty-something bachelor. They just weren't going to do that." The numerous slide-show presentations George and Martha did in people's homes throughout the winter months were more than a way to market trips – they were an opportunity to sell themselves.

The first trip, in the summer of 1966, offered a seven-week itinerary in Europe. Forty-four students signed up, far more than expected. At most, George, Martha, and Sidney had figured they might get twenty or thirty. Realizing that so many teenagers would be too much for the three of them to manage safely, Sidney enlisted a law-school buddy, Bob McDermott, to be their baggage boy. "We were in third year sitting in the back row of one of those amphitheatres, in a tax class, and I asked him if he would like to go all expenses paid to Europe for the summer," remembers Sidney. As things turned out, Bob was a great fit for the new team.

George and Sidney had learned from Dick and Stan how to wring the most fun out of a European journey. Rather than reinvent the wheel, they emulated the basic formula of a Gibb-Macfarlane trip but introduced a few important changes they felt would make for an even better experience. Whereas the Gibb-Macfarlane trips had started and finished with a five- or six-day non-stop crossing of the cold, windy, and often rough North Atlantic, the Butterfield & Robinson trip opted to fly the students home from London. The journey over was a warm and sunny ten-day cruise from New York to Naples aboard the elegant *Leonardo da Vinci* ocean liner. With stops along the way in Madeira, Gibraltar, Majorca, and Sicily, the southern route was more interesting and less likely to trigger seasickness. Many of the students sat out on the deck drinking beer at all hours of the night, Bob recalls – though in Sidney's recollection Bob was the one who helped supply the beer.

··················
ABOVE
*All decked out
on the first trip*

RIGHT
*The Leonardo's
proud prow*

BELOW
*Connecting the
dots of the first
student trip*

LEFT
Afoot in the Alps

RIGHT
*Students awash
in sunshine on
the French Riviera*

Serendipity

It's tempting to assume that the first B&R trip was a triumph because it was meticulously planned, with each moment precision crafted and every detail buttoned down months in advance. But it wasn't really like that. On the day the trip started the itinerary had a few holes. Some hotel bookings had not yet been made and the routing and activities for each day weren't completely sorted out.

As Sidney, Martha, and Bob travelled with the students by ship from New York to Naples, George found himself alone on a flight to Germany wondering where they would do the week of biking they had listed in the brochure. He saw promising green space south of Munich on the Michelin maps, so he headed down there as soon as he landed in search of roads to bike – and bikes to rent.

When he stepped off the train in the pretty town of Starnberg, he discovered that a spectacular bike trail ran along the shore of the nearby lake. He also met Herr Veden at the train station, who suggested a couple of places to stay along the way *and* agreed to rent him forty-three single-speed bikes. He couldn't believe his luck.

Once on the ground in Europe, the itinerary followed a familiar and proven pattern of urban and rural exploration, diverse modes of transportation, and plenty of physical activity. They hiked and took cog trains in the mountains of Switzerland, floated the canals of Venice by gondola, steamed up the Rhine on riverboats, and biked through the Bavarian countryside. And just like the Gibb-Macfarlane trips, the students visited the cultural capitals of Western Europe – Rome, Florence, Munich, Paris, and London.

The key difference was that Butterfield & Robinson put a much stronger emphasis on the opportunity to learn. They wanted the experience to transform the students. In George's words: "We made a big effort to make the trip more educational about the culture of Europe. All those kids would come back wanting to study art or archaeology. We tried to inspire them with energy and enthusiasm." With Sidney and Martha delivering cultural talks and leading all the guided tours along the way, it was possible to weave a coherent story from Rome to London, start to finish. It gave the students a comprehensive view that put historical *and* modern Europe in context.

Not surprisingly, the students had a great time and were dazzled by what they saw, tasted, and experienced. That's not to say everything was silky smooth from beginning to end. Less than an hour into the trip, as the group was travelling by train from Toronto to New York to meet the ship, Martha noticed that one of the boys was acting strangely – feverishly checking his watch every few seconds. Realizing he was emotionally unfit to continue with the trip, they called his parents and George flew back to Toronto with him the next morning. At the end of the cruise, a day before disembarking in Naples, Sidney discovered that two of the students had smuggled

···················

RIGHT
*Sidney enlightens
a group in Rome*

FAR RIGHT
*Martha conducting
a tour at the Art
Gallery of Ontario*

NEXT
*Taking in the
long view at
Lake Starnberg*

But there was one other problem: George had no accommodation for one night of the bike journey. He didn't panic, kept his cool, and just kept looking around. Eventually he found a farmer who agreed to let the group sleep in his barn. It could have been a tough sell and a disastrous night, but George marshalled some magic. Bob remembers what happened when the group rolled into the farmyard a few days later: "He gathered everybody together and said we've got this great adventure. I have this barn for us tonight and we're going to have dinner, music, and dancing, and then we'll sleep on the hay in the barn. Everybody was happy about this arrangement, cheering and saying it was terrific." Ever aware of their responsibility as chaperones (but equally keen to keep the policing playful), Martha anointed one of the students as the chief morality officer.

That wasn't the only time on the trip they pulled a rabbit out of a hat. Just one week before there had been another gap in the accommodation roster. The B&R brochure suggested the students would "stay in one or two of the great hotels of the world." Alas, nothing had been reserved. Bob remembers Sidney turning to him in Venice, saying: "We're in the Italian Lakes in a few nights and we don't have anywhere to stay. Go and see if you can find us something." It was the sort of unorthodox yet trusting and wonderful move B&R came to perfect. Bob drove off and, a few hours later, pulled into the parking lot of the Grand Hotel des Iles Borromées to ask for directions.

marijuana aboard the ship. Alarmed that they did not appreciate the criminal implications of taking drugs into Europe and worried that the sniffer dogs would be waiting at customs, he had them flush their cache down the toilet and wipe their luggage clean with a damp cloth.

Notwithstanding some teenage mischief, the students stayed out of serious trouble and willingly followed their leaders. "We were like the Pied Piper of Hamelin," Martha remembers: "If we said come here, they came. There was no rebellion, and everybody did everything we suggested. They loved it – whenever we run into them now they say how much we opened their lives."

Back in Toronto at the living-room-floor office, the trio sat down to see how they'd fared financially. Everyone pulled out leftover stashes of traveller's cheques and cash: German marks, French francs, British sterling, Italian lira – piles of paper in every currency of the trip. "I remember distributing it and saying, 'One for you, one for you, and one for me,'" says Martha. "So we divvied up this cash, though we had no idea how much was there. And then we found we had actually made $12,000 on that trip – more money than any of us had ever dreamed of." When someone asked, "Should we do this again?" George shot back, "Are you kidding!"

Set on the shores of Lake Maggiore, with six storeys of neoclassical heft and five shiny stars, it was a grand hotel of the most luxurious order. It was decidedly not the kind of place a group of students would normally stay. But Bob had orders to find a hotel and, after negotiating a group rate with the manager, he called George, Sidney, and Martha to discuss the option. At $15 per room per night "it was a real splurge," recalls George, "but we had to do it." After the students checked in, the leaders decided they should have a toga party. "So all these kids come down with their sheets, and we put tables on the lawn," says Bob. "The hotel had never seen anything like it, but, being Italian, they loved it."

By leaving space in the itinerary and not micro organizing everything in advance, George, Martha, and Sidney let serendipity slip into the moment. They knew exactly how to harness it.

They quickly decided to offer essentially the same trip the following summer, in 1967. And again in 1968 – this time with nearly seventy students signed up. Butterfield & Robinson was slowly gaining momentum, though they had no long-term plans beyond the upcoming season. For the first three years it was a fun and fruitful summer hobby, nothing more.

Besides, they had other responsibilities the rest of the year, and not all of them were able to guide every summer. Once Sidney finished his law degree, he worked full time for a short stint at his father's law firm. Martha was completing her master's in fine art at the University of Toronto while working part-time in the education department at the Art Gallery of Ontario. And George, heeding his father's advice to launch a real career, accepted a job at Patino Mining Corporation as assistant to the president. He and Martha were hoping to have children soon and, nearing thirty, they thought it was time to get serious.

At Patino, George quickly earned the confidence of his boss, Erskine Carter, who made him responsible for legal issues and involved him in special projects. George was on the corporate track. Nevertheless, he managed to slip out of the office most lunches to check up on things at the Boiler Room (a restaurant he and a friend had started while still in law school) or race home to see if there were any phone messages about Butterfield & Robinson trips.

```
                    LP
         ¢CCC-RX

         RXONE/LRA2105 RNC051
         GCLB HL CXTO 027
         TORONTO ONT 27 18 1155P


         LT
         BUTTERFIELD AND ROBINSON MAPLETON HOTEL 39 COVENTRYSTR
         LONDONENG


         CONFUCIUS SAY MUCH BOOZE ON BR VERY GOOD FOR FAREWELL DINNER
         AND FOR BIG HEADACHE ON PLANE
                GEORGE


         COL 39

         CCC-RX
```

7.45a

....
ABOVE
*A philosophical
trip report*

RIGHT
*An arch gives way
to daylight at the
Colosseum*

This juggling routine went on for more than a year until a mid-summer morning in 1968 when George saw a newspaper article announcing that the Patino Mining Corporation was being taken over by Occidental Petroleum. He marched into Erskine's office. "I was upset and felt he'd betrayed me by not keeping me up with developments," says George. "Erskine pushed back and said, 'I didn't know either.'" George saw red: "Oh, so that's how the world works: the owners sit in Paris, we do all the work, and they decide our fate." He resigned and left Patino a few weeks later. George wanted to be self-sufficient, to invent his own life.

When Mrs. Robinson heard that her beloved son-in-law had decided to focus full-time on Butterfield & Robinson, she responded with typical vigour. "You're what?" she fired back. "You're going to be a travel agent?" George wasn't thinking of it as a conventional travel agency, but he was immediately chuffed at the label. Mrs. Robinson wasn't done, however. "You're an entrepreneur," she continued, " – and entrepreneurs are rats!" It was a stinging assessment, but nothing was going to break George's new stride. He doubled down, determined to transform Butterfield & Robinson from a summer venture into a real company.

The first move was to get a proper office. They leased a space on Bay Street (Toronto's answer to Wall Street), bought a coffee machine, and hired Butterfield & Robinson's first full-time employees – Mary Essl, an Austrian who regularly made strudel for the office, and David Young, an aspiring young writer with friendly eyes and a quick tongue. Martha, drawing on her experience at the architectural firm, finessed the design in a clean, colourful, contemporary style – sleek and impressive. When Sidney walked into the office for the first time he exclaimed, "We'll never see a dividend again." It was a well-founded comment.

Arctic lures students with promise of

This summer, 18 young travellers will set off on an adventure they will never forget —a trip to the Canadian Arctic, July 5 to 26.

They will fly from Montreal to Frobisher Bay, for their first stopover. From there, they go to Pangnirtung, and board Eskimo boats for a five-day trip up Clearwater Fjord to join the Eskimos in a caribou hunt and to harpoon beluga whales. They go from there to Resolute and to Grise Fjord on Ellesmere Island, Canada's most northerly settlement, where they will go out onto sea ice with Eskimos and their dogs to hunt square-flipper seal, walrus or Polar bear. Then they go to Hall Lake and from there return home.

The trip is arranged by Butterfield and Robinson Travel, specialists in student travel. They promise only hard travel and discomfort, with plenty of excitement thrown in.

The party will travel by charter plane, and will camp most of the time, except in Pangnirtung, Igloolik, Resolute and Grise Fiord, where Northwest Territories officials have arranged accommodation in Government buildings which are vacant in summer.

Arctic travel is expensive; cost of the trip is $1,700 from Montreal. "Ten years from now," say the organizers, "it will not be as costly—nor as exciting."

For information, call Butterfield and Robinson Travel, Essex House, Suite 209, 185 Bay St., Toronto.

discomfort and excitement on sea ice

After years of operating B&R out of the living room at minimal cost, the business suddenly had significant overheads. As George puts it, "Revenue wasn't really supporting all the expenses." The student trips were doing reasonably well, with three European departures running in the summer of 1969 (one led by Bob McDermott, another by Sidney, and the third by George and Martha). In addition, an adventurous new trip to the Canadian Arctic was launched to test the icy waters and see if students would find caribou and whale hunting on remote Ellesmere Island as appealing as splashing around in the Trevi Fountain. A handful did, but not enough to justify running the trip again the following summer. Butterfield & Robinson's business was growing, albeit a little too slowly to keep pace with the dream and the overheads.

Adding to the pressure was the mortgage for a new house George and Martha had purchased. Martha, moreover, was pregnant with their first child. Preternaturally laid-back and slow to ruffle, George was nonetheless feeling the heat. "All of a sudden I'm going to work full time to make the company a world brand and it's tough sledding," he recalls. "The sweat was starting to hit the brow because I realized I wasn't getting a paycheque as I had before; and David, who was born in 1970, was coming along." It was crunch time.

Determined to find or develop a niche to call its own, Butterfield & Robinson was ready and willing to try almost anything

RE; PROPOSAL TO THE CANADIAN IMPERIAL BANK OF COMMERCE

THESE PAPERS ARE ORIGINALS AND THE

PAGES MISSING TO THIS PROPOSAL

ARE WITH THE PROPOSAL TO THE

BANK OF ~~MONTREAL~~ NOVA SCOTIA.

And so began a period of relentless experimentation and wild creativity. Determined to find or develop a niche to call its own, Butterfield & Robinson was ready and willing to try almost anything. No matter how audaciously large or ridiculously improbable the idea, the trio were willing to chase it down and give it a whirl. Sooner or later they would hit the jackpot. They simply had to keep looking.

In search of big numbers, one of the first places George turned to was the Bank of Nova Scotia. He wasn't looking for a loan so much as a partner. In a detailed proposal to the bank, George suggested that "a joint venture company (Scotia Tours Limited) be formed to plan, organize, market and conduct interesting and exciting package tour vacations throughout the world. Butterfield & Robinson would provide management for Scotia Tours, and the Bank of Nova Scotia would make its branches available for the sale of the tours." In short, George wanted to open mini travel agencies in bank branches all across the country: "I saw myself going from one location to five thousand overnight," he recalls. It was a big dream, and George worked his tail off to make the deal happen. Meeting after meeting he chased the dream until a decision finally reached the board level.

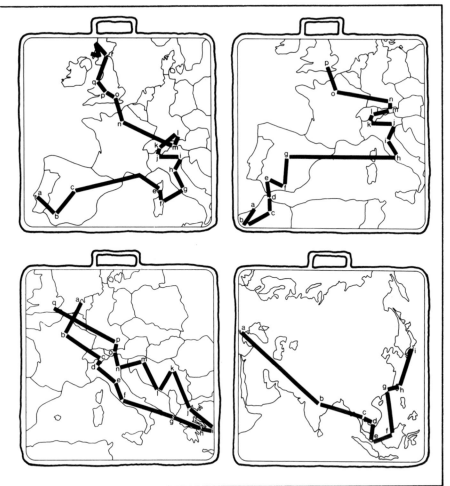

Travel is Our Bag

Butterfield & Robinson
Trips for Students
Summer 1970

These trips are for those who expect more from travel than bus rides, guided tours, prepaid meals and conventional hotel accommodation.

These trips are organized to the extent that organization is desirable, yet independence and freedom are stressed at all times. We strive to develop in people a sense for the art of travelling on their own.

Butterfield & Robinson,
Suite 1604, 330 Bay Street,
Toronto 105, Ontario.
Telephone 364-9248
(Area Code 416)

He was beside himself with expectations.

After the board meeting, George got a call from the bank president asking him to come to his office for a chat. "You are a talented person," the president began. "You put together something really compelling and interesting. We love the idea, but can I just tell you something? Little companies and big companies don't mix well, and so we can't do it." George felt he had lost everything, but he wasn't prepared to let go of the dream just yet. He turned to the Canadian Imperial Bank of Commerce, one of the other large banks, and pitched the same idea. Again the proposal eventually made its way to the very top, and again he got a call from the chairman with the same message. "So I guess it finally sunk in," says George, "that joint ventures between big companies and little companies just don't work out."

Other ventures bore more fruit. With the help of Marie Macfarlane (a long-time teacher and Stan Macfarlane's wife), Butterfield & Robinson set up the Canadian Travel & Study Foundation (CTSF), a non-profit organization that took large numbers of students to Europe for short, inexpensive trips with an educational slant. The fees were modest, but the program helped to keep the company

Butterfield & Robinson European Trips for Students. Summer 1972

busy and afloat. In the spring of 1972 CTSF arranged for nearly a thousand students to travel to Paris and Grenoble for the March break. George and Martha, who were living in Paris for the year, gave these mass trips a touch of B&R intimacy by arranging for each student to have dinner with a French family. The CTSF experience convinced George, Martha, and Sidney that B&R could play a larger role in connecting North American students with longer-term study and cultural learning in Europe. The following year the company developed a plan to buy and operate a school in Grenoble, but the project was scrapped because of the overwhelming start-up costs.

Sidney, who had also been in the B&R daily fold since early 1969 (just a few months after George had started full-time), worked hard to push the company toward profitability. While George and Martha were living in Paris, working on B&R's expansion ideas, Sidney ran the Toronto office, managing the development of the student trips, opening travel agencies, and developing contacts with cultural organizations with which to partner.

But the challenges of shared control and divergent views on growth gradually created tension between the two male principals. In one pivotal conversation Sidney expressed concern over the amount of money being spent on the brochure and marketing materials. George responded, "Without sales we have no business." "Yes," Sidney agreed, but "if we lose $50 on each sale we make we won't have a business either."

**Art Gallery of Ontario
Art Tour of
Iran and Afghanistan
April 16 - May 4, 1975**
Organized by the Volunteer Committee.

"It wasn't our happiest time together," remarks George, "and that was because we were both big boys in a tiny little office without much revenue." Not long after George and Martha's return from Paris, Sidney, who had always been attracted to law, decided to join Torys LLP, as it's now called, where he practised law for thirty years and played a major role in managing this prestigious firm. "I always thought I was going to be a lawyer," says Sidney. "My father was a partner in a law firm, and that was the role model I had."

From 1973 onward George was unquestionably the driving force behind the company, but Sidney had not lost his affection for B&R and stayed involved both as an owner and an adviser. In 1973 he led a trip to Guatemala and the Yucatan, one of the first off the European continent for B&R. Others followed. In 1975, while Mao Zedong was still alive and the Cultural Revolution was in full swing, Sidney led the first trip to China; three years later, just before the fall of the Shah, he guided the first trip to Iran; and in the early eighties he guided the first walking trip in the Italian Lake District. Sidney's commitment was twofold: to law/Torys and to his family travel company. Jim Tory, the leader of Torys LLP, even encouraged

"I always thought it was like theatre"

Sidney's travel passion, believing it would make him a better and more thoughtful lawyer in the end.

With so much creative energy and enthusiasm pumping through the business, B&R continued to experiment and expand. The original European itinerary had morphed into multiple versions and included numerous options to the British Isles, Belgium, Holland, Greece, Turkey, Russia, and Morocco. As George's right-hand man, David Young was hitting his stride and becoming a masterful jack of many trades – researching trips, guiding trips, promoting trips, writing materials for trips, and dreaming up new trips. Most important, he was helping B&R find the narrative for a summer experience that would transform students' lives. "I always thought it was like theatre," says Young – a telling comment from a man who would go on to become an award-winning playwright.

The defining moment of the trip was a victory lap around the Arc de Triomphe in Paris

The student trips were finding a rhythm, and every year the underlying details got tighter and tighter. The idea was to remove chance from the equation as much as possible so that guides would be better prepared to seize the magical moments of serendipity. In all the trips, the week or more of biking, for example, seemed to enhance the overall drama and enjoyment of the experience. The bicycle seemed a perfect vehicle for the brand of fun B&R sought to deliver. So in the summer of 1973 the company offered its first all-biking student trip, a forty-five-day journey from Vienna to Paris. Young, one of the guides on the trip, remembers: "This was the first time we decided to go right across Europe. There were places where we had to cross mountain ranges, so we took a train, but otherwise it was the bikes. There was no van with luggage – we were just a bunch of kids with *panniers*. It was really really fun, really a gas." The defining moment of the trip was a victory lap around the Arc de Triomphe in Paris. George was there with a Super 8mm video camera to capture the excitement as twenty-five kids, surrounded by happily honking cars, circled the iconic monument. "The kids were over the moon," says Young. "It blew our minds that we could do it."

Never one to fade into the background, Martha, now the mother of two very young children (David and Nathalie), miraculously found the time and energy to continue guiding trips and developing new programs. As a guide, she had a talent for pulling the students into her orbit. Richard Meech took his first B&R trip, a high school

ABOVE
*A river runs
around it in
Northern Canada*

BELOW
*Illustrations
from a
Polar Trippers
brochure*

graduation present from his parents, in 1972: "My leader that year was Martha Butterfield – you can't get better than that," he says. "Everyone arrived at the Rome airport all bleary-eyed and wondering what we were doing. We didn't speak Italian, and we didn't know if we wanted to be with all these other students. There was Martha on the microphone at the front of the bus going into Rome at eight o'clock in the morning, welcoming us and telling us about ancient Rome and how much fun we were going to have. I immediately felt relaxed because she clearly knew what she was doing and put everybody at ease. She gave everyone the sense that we were here for an adventure and we were going to see some extraordinary things." The spark jumped again: the following summer Richard returned to be a guide himself.

Europe was still the focus of B&R's business, but George continued to scan the horizon, looking for a gold strike. As a proud Canadian, he once again turned his gaze to the country's vast and under-explored wilderness region to the north. For a large group of top donors to the World Wildlife Fund (WWF), B&R created a trip around Baker

Running Rapids

2.8 million litres (750,000 gallons) of water pour over Niagara Falls every second. At the bottom of the falls the surface of the Niagara River is calm enough for the iconic *Maid of the Mist* sightseeing boat to ply the water, but a mile or so downstream the tremendous volume is pinched into a deep gorge. At that point, in the Whirlpool Rapids, the river narrows to as little as 60 metres (200 feet) and turns into a roiling, broiling, frothy mess. Standing waves regularly reach 4 to 6 metres (15 to 20 feet). The white-water classification system labels it a Class VI rapid – the extreme end of the spectrum, virtually impossible to navigate.

Drawn to the challenge and opportunity of offering an experience that would be unique and wildly adventurous, George

Lake, in Canada's Hudson Bay region. The success of the trip inspired B&R, in collaboration with George's friend David Ross, an avid outdoorsman, to launch a standalone program called Polar Trippers. It offered a few northern wilderness excursions – canoeing journeys on the Dawson and Mackenzie rivers and white-water rafting on the Coppermine and Nahanni. These trips were unique, innovative adventures, but they failed to attract much interest. After limping along for a few years in the mid to late seventies, the Polar Trippers program melted away. David also helped George develop a grand scheme for white-water rafting in the Niagara Gorge – but that one ended in tragedy, one of the darkest days in the company's history.

All the while that B&R was experimenting with ground-breaking trip ideas, George still held to the belief that the company had the potential to become Canada's largest mainstream travel agency. Gradually the dream gained momentum. By 1980 B&R had five offices – a main office at 330 Bay Street and four branch agencies (two in Toronto, one in Montreal, and one in Calgary). "I thought the Butterfield & Robinson name was catching on and would lend a certain credibility," he recalls. And that's what happened. "We had

....
LEFT
*The Grider riding
the Niagara River*

BELOW
*An early
branch office*

really good people running really good businesses." The travel agencies were able to handle a high volume of flight and hotel bookings, providing B&R with an operational platform to pursue and test a wide variety of ideas.

And test they did. There were university alumni association tours to Hong Kong, Yugoslavia, Barbados, and Cuba. Corporate incentive trips such as the one they did for General Motors, which included an evening at the Playboy Club on the shores of Lake Geneva. Spring-break trips to Club Med in Mexico, Whistler, and Aspen. Large group trips to China, Guatemala, New Orleans, and Senegal for the Ontario Teachers' Federation. Seminars in Vancouver for the Acupuncture Society of Canada. Packages to the World Ice Hockey Championships in the Soviet Union – and a year later, the Olympics in Moscow. Getaway weekends to New York City for supporters of the National Ballet of Canada, cross-country and downhill ski trips in North America and Europe, and even a two-day dance tour around Toronto "featuring a performance by Rafael Nunoz's 4-piece South American Band."

The profit margins were slim and, for the most part, the spirit of the agency trips did not jive with B&R's underlying ethos. George remembers the corporate incentive trips being particularly tedious: "I didn't like the fact that you couldn't be yourself – somebody else was sitting on you and making you compromise," he recalls. The

set up Niagara Gorge River Trips Inc. in 1975. He wasn't the first to have the idea of developing a commercially viable white-water rafting operation on the Niagara River. A few years before, George Grider, a retired U.S. submarine commander, and his business associate William Wendell had tried to do something similar but had abandoned the project when they were unable to develop a raft robust enough to withstand the intensity of the rapids.

Backed by investors, George resurrected the dream in the early seventies by turning to the respected engineering firm Calspan (formerly Cornell Aeronautical Laboratory) to design the ideal vessel and to the French firm Zodiac to build it. After much research and considerable cost, he took delivery of a mammoth inflatable raft with enormous outrigger pontoons. At 10.6 by 8.2 metres (35 by 27 feet), it was like nothing the Niagara River, or any river, had ever seen. To pilot the raft, he hired two highly experienced white-water guides from Colorado. George had done his homework and, after several successful test runs, it seemed that the Niagara Gorge had finally been conquered.

On a gorgeous late summer day in August 1975, the *Grider*, as George named the raft, slipped into the river for its eleventh test run. With twenty-nine people aboard (one shy of capacity), the raft was running with the biggest load yet. George wasn't on board, but he'd invited several friends and colleagues to join in the fun,

Shipwreck Holidays
Butterfield & Robinson Travel

....
PREVIOUS
Martha enjoys a
magic moment
in the
port of Bodrum

LEFT
Prospecting for
adventurous
travellers

including Stan and Marie Macfarlane, David Ross, Richard Meech, and the Zodiac engineer who had overseen the project. Everyone was excited and expecting another flawless run.

"Basically, what I remember is that there wasn't much going on," recalls Richard. "The boat was so big it was just lumbering over the rapids. Some waves began to splash up and shower us with water, but we were all dressed for that. Then all of a sudden we went over one wave and into a deep trough. We started climbing up another wave, kind of crawled up, and went 'whoosh' down into this next trough. I thought, 'Wow, this is getting pretty scary.' We plunged into another trough, and as we began to climb the wave, it kept growing taller and taller. All we had in front of us was this wall of rising dark-green water. For a moment everything was silent – and then, suddenly, we were all flipped into the furious water."

The raft was upside down. Many of the passengers managed to grab onto ropes on the side of the raft, but a handful were swept into the violent rapids. Richard was one of them. "The tough part for me was realizing I was alone... maybe I was the only one. I was moving fast, about 30 miles per hour, and I was surrounded by waves and couldn't even see the shore." After being pushed under several times, Richard's life jacket popped him back to the surface. Eventually he was able to make his way to land.

Three of the passengers weren't as lucky. David Ross (George's partner in the rafting venture), Julia Martinez (a travel agent at B&R), and Anthony Sawczyk (a young rafting enthusiast from the Niagara area) lost their lives that afternoon. "One of them was

"Who else could imagine charging an outrageous amount of money to starve everybody to death?"

extreme cost-sensitivity was also off-putting. When reminded of a contract B&R won because they included 1.5-ounce drinks, not the 1.25-ounce drinks offered by the competition, George shakes his head in dismay. Nevertheless, the travel-agency revenue helped pay the monthly bills and allowed George to keep experimenting with other more innovative and fun ventures.

Of all the wild and crazy ideas B&R tried, none were as outlandish as Shipwreck Holidays. Although by the mid-seventies Gibb-Macfarlane had ceased to operate trips, George and Sidney remained close friends with their former bosses and mentors and regularly saw them socially. As they always had, Dick and George loved to talk business and bounce ideas around. Out sailing on Lake Ontario one afternoon in the fall of 1977, Dick pitched George on his latest and greatest notion – to "shipwreck" a group of like-minded travellers on a beautiful tropical island. It was the sort of idea that only an innovative adventurer like Dick would float, and only a creative entrepreneur like George would seize.

For $399, B&R's Shipwreck Holiday included return flights between Toronto and Nassau (Bahamas), boat transfers to an idyllic deserted island, a bucket, a sheet of plastic, and a book of matches. Neither food nor water was included, but participants were taught basic survival techniques so they could condense their own water (using the bucket and plastic) and catch or forage enough to eat. Fifteen people signed up for the trip. "There must have been some other island you could walk to at very low tide," says George, "because this one guy decided after four days that he'd had enough and walked across to a hotel." The trip didn't get rave reviews and was never repeated. It did, however, sitting in front of me, one beside me, and one behind me," recollects Richard with sadness and disbelief.

Reeling from the shock, George's first impulse was to call Sidney, who was, by complete and ironic coincidence, in the middle of a business meeting with Dick Meech, Richard's father, when the phone rang. They spoke briefly about what had happened, and Sidney relayed to Dick the news that Richard was unharmed.

Against conventional legal advice, George went on television that evening to explain what had happened and offer his profound sympathy. The Niagara's Daredevil Hall of Fame wanted to buy the raft to display in the museum, but George turned away in disgust. The whole experience was a tremendous personal blow for him. To this day it is illegal to raft down the Niagara Gorge.

earn B&R the top prize in the *International Herald Tribune*'s creative travel awards. "Who else," the citation read, "could imagine charging an outrageous amount of money to starve everybody to death?"

Throughout the seventies the company tried again and again to develop a business focused on educating students abroad. Inspired by her experience at Neuchâtel Junior College in Switzerland, Martha in 1978 championed the development of a program called Études à Nice, which would cater to Canadian students who wanted to learn French and absorb the culture. The idea was simple. Students from the province of Ontario would spend a year in Nice to complete their grade 12 equivalent, live with a local family, and attend a *lycée* (a local French high school). Richard Meech, who was in Paris completing a graduate scholarship, jumped at the chance to start the program. The venture did get off the ground, but barely, and it lasted for only a few years. Not enough students had an appetite for such a local experience. "I think it must have been too intensive, *too* authentic," recalls Martha with a whiff of disappointment.

While many of the ventures B&R tried in the first decade and a half of existence did well enough, one of the most successful was a series of trips, conceived and operated for the Art Gallery of Ontario (AGO) and the Royal Ontario Museum (ROM), two of Canada's top cultural institutions. With them, B&R not only found partners who cared as much about art and culture as they did but also had long lists of

RIGHT
Dr. Douglas Bryce leading the way on a trip for the Royal Ontario Museum

OPPOSITE TOP
M.G. Eaton and Dudley and Deborah Butterfield (George's mum and dad) following Ulysses

OPPOSITE BOTTOM
Badges for Sid and Midge Robinson (Sidney and Martha's parents)

affluent members – a large pool of potential travellers. Unlike the student tours, the institutional trips were short, profitable, and upscale. Beginning in 1972 with a trip for the AGO called the Cathedrals & Châteaux of Île de France & the Loire Valley, B&R developed a handful of imaginatively themed and evocatively titled journeys every year: a Maya art tour through Guatemala and Mexico; a Viking adventure to Iceland, Norway, and Denmark; a visit to Irish houses and castles. The trips were interesting to put together, fun to operate, and extremely well received by adult travellers looking for something fresh.

Buoyed by the instant success of the programs and inspired by Ernle Bradford's book *Ulysses Found* (a story of the author's seven-year sailing journey through the Mediterranean in search of proof that Homer's *Odyssey* was based on fact, not fiction), George saw an opportunity to raise the stakes. Wouldn't it be cool, he thought, to charter a ship and retrace the supposed trail of Ulysses? In 1976 B&R put together their biggest trip yet for the AGO, Follow Ulysses: A Mediterranean Art Cruise, a 120-passenger trip aboard the *Stella Oceanis*. "We had to make a down payment to secure the ship and we had to mortgage our house to do it," George recollects. "Everything was on the line." Bradford agreed to join the trip as a guest expert, and by the time the ship sailed it was completely sold out. The risk paid off and landed B&R an alluring jackpot.

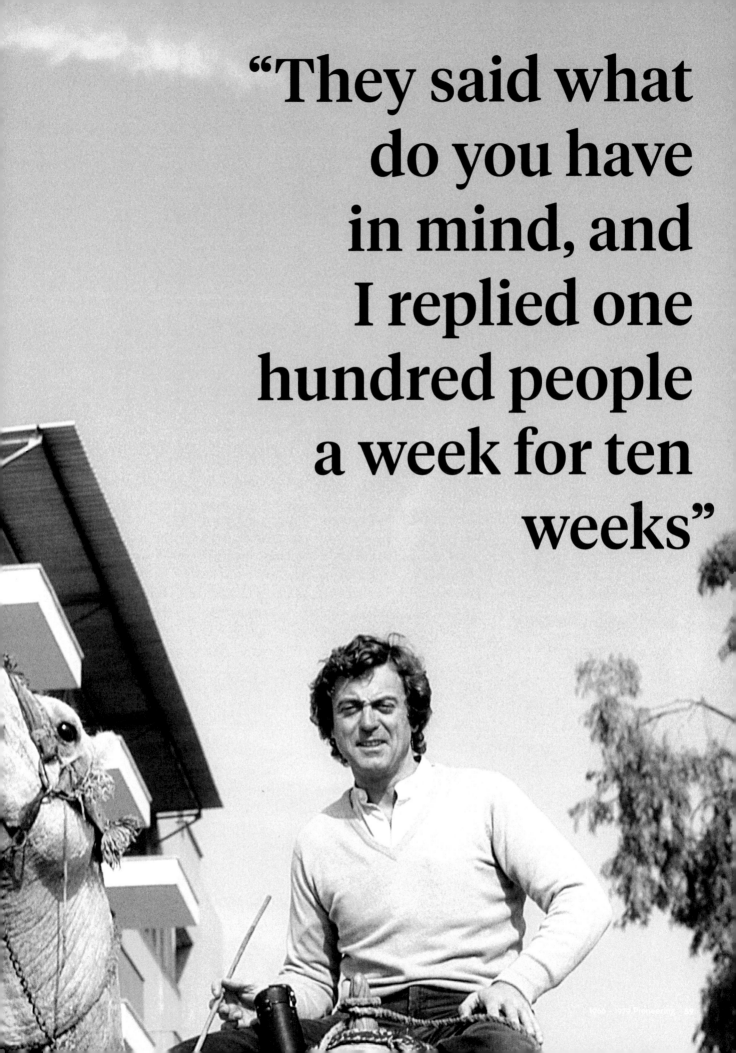

"They said what do you have in mind, and I replied one hundred people a week for ten weeks"

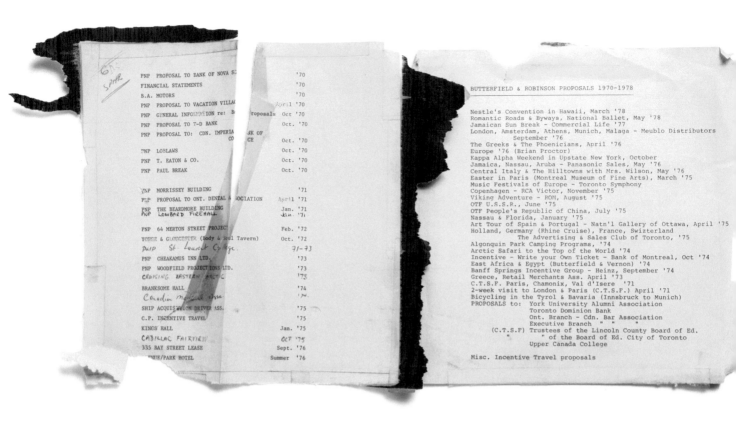

Uncluttered TUT

....
PREVIOUS
*George atop a
camel in Cairo*

TOP
*A long, long list
along the way*

ABOVE
*Graphic from a
notecard telling
the world
about B&R's
Tutankhamun trip*

A few years later, inspiration and success struck again. The wildly popular touring exhibit, *The Treasures of Tutankhamun*, blazed through Toronto in 1979 and triggered a massive interest in Egypt. George approached the AGO with an idea for a one-week journey to Cairo, Aswan, and Luxor: "They said what do you have in mind, and I replied one hundred people a week for ten weeks – one thousand people. They looked at me askance. Even now when I think about it I shudder – one thousand people! That was a lot of travellers in a ten-week period for our little company. So I called up British Airways and reserved ten weeks, one hundred people a week. When the package hit the market it went crazy." A thousand people signed up for the trip. But when George called British Airways to give them the names, they confessed they hadn't actually blocked off that many seats. In the end, B&R was able to scrape together enough seats to send nearly 700 people to Egypt.

That's the kind of pattern B&R established in its pioneering years. Even with tremendous effort and relentless experimentation, they were never quite able to pin the tail on the donkey. "I'll tell you that it was very tough to make a living; it was hard to make ends meet," says George. "I was working like a dog but not making any money. I was just flat out trying everything." Still, there was no giving up. Like any true entrepreneur, George was convinced a breakthrough idea was just around the corner. In his gut, he knew the world was ready for a fresh approach to travel – the love child of creativity, comfort, and activity. But he could not see yet how to deliver it.

All Over the Map

Butterfield & Robinson has covered a lot of ground since 1966 – over 100 countries. Even more amazing than the number of places B&R travellers have biked and walked is how often and how early they've made fresh tracks.

Added to the Mix
Number of new countries added per era.

67
New Countries

18
New Countries

CANADA
1969

GREENLAND
1977

ICELAND
1975

NORWA
1974

UNITED KINGDOM
1966

NETHERLAND
1970

IRELAND
1967

BELG
1970

UNITED STATES
1973

BERMUDA
1974

BAHAMAS
1978

SPAIN
1966

FRANCE
1966

LUXEMBO
1972

CUBA
1976

VIRGIN ISLANDS
1977

MONACO
1971

MAL
197

GUATEMALA
1974

BELIZE
1993

JAMAICA
1989

PORTUGAL
1969

MOROCCO
1969

MEXICO
1973

HAITI
1981

BARBADOS
1972

NICARAGUA
2012

VENEZUELA
1664

TUNISIA
1969

ITALY
1966

COSTA RICA
1982

PANAMA
1982

COLOMBIA
1977

BRAZIL
1977

ECUADOR
1975

LYBIA
2007

BOLIVIA
1978

SENEGAL
1977

PERU
1975

BOTSWAN
1988

ARGENTINA
1982

NAMIBIA
2008

CHILE
1995

URUGUAY
2011

SOUTH AFRICA
1983

Note: Map not to scale. Country names and / or borders may have changed.

FINLAND
1969

POLAND
1976

AFGHANISTAN
1975

RUSSIA
1971

JAPAN
1970

DEN
81

DENMARK
1972

UKRAINE
2011

IRAN
1975

CZECH REPUBLIC
1968

SLOVAKIA
1968

RMANY
1966

AUSTRIA
1966

CHINA
1974

LIECHTENSTEIN
1973

TURKEY
1971

TZERLAND
1966

SERBIA
1970

HUNGARY
1987

NEPAL
1979

BHUTAN
2001

TAIWAN
1970

LEBANON
2010

SYRIA
2009

LAOS
2004

CROATIA
1970

OMAN
2009

HONG KONG
1970

SLOVENIA
1970

GREECE
1969

INDIA
1970

MYANMAR
2000

VIETNAM
1998

BANGLADESH
1982

EGYPT
1975

ISRAEL
1971

SRI LANKA
1984

SINGAPORE
1970

CAMBODIA
1970

THAILAND
1970

RWANDA
2012

JORDAN
1979

MALAYSIA
1970

LAWI
006

UGANDA
2004

KENYA
1975

INDONESIA
1980

PAPUA NEW GUINEA
1983

TANZANIA
1974

ZAMBIA
1988

AUSTRALIA
1983

NEW ZEALAND
1985

ZIMBABWE
1988

THE
STRUDEL
BOOT
(1972)

"*The first condition of understanding a foreign country is to smell it.*"

RUDYARD KIPLING

3

1980
-
1993

The Bicycle Hits the Bullseye

Ideas are catnip to George: he can't get enough of them, and he has endless energy to bat them around. So when Richard Meech walked into George's office on a June day in 1980 with a new idea he wanted to discuss, the welcome was warm. For seven years Richard had been working on and off for B&R – guiding student tours in Europe each summer, helping to develop the Études à Nice study program, and living in Cairo for the four previous months as B&R's point person for the Tutankhamun trips. He'd proven himself a capable and creative trip planner, a loyal and trusted friend, as someone who delivered.

George was ready to listen.

"I've noticed something over the last few summers when I return home from Europe with the students," Richard began. "At the airport, I meet their parents, and amid all the greeting and hugging and crying and laughing I often hear a request: 'When are you going to offer a trip like that for us?'"

George looked at him stony-eyed. He was polite, waiting for Richard to finish.

"I think we're missing a *big* market here," Richard continued earnestly. "We should offer adult bicycle trips in Europe, but more luxurious than the student version, of course. And shorter too, only one week. We'll transport their luggage in a van while they bike all day, eat in nice restaurants, and stay in good hotels. We'll organize a few vintage wine tastings and a couple of town walks, and people will have a great trip. That's it, very simple."

"We did not have a single taker on that trip. Not one person booked"

George was nodding his head, a gesture Richard took to be a positive sign. He pressed on.

"I say we try one trip, and that should be in Burgundy this September during the wine harvest. We'll call it Bicycling in Burgundy. Who knows, this could grow into a whole new series of trips!"

George was silent. He looked at the ceiling for a moment, then, putting his hands together, tapped the tips of his fingers lightly. He spoke slowly.

"Been there, done that, Richard. It doesn't work."

George was partly right. Eight years earlier, in 1972, B&R had tested the idea of an adult biking trip. In partnership with Lufthansa, the airline they used for all the student trips, they put together a brochure offering a one-week adult bicycling tour in southern Germany. They planned to stay at the same hotels as the students did and priced the trip modestly at $199 per person for a standard room, or $249 for a superior room. The brochures were sent to the office of every Lufthansa representative in Canada and the United States – ultimately reaching an audience of tens of thousands of potential travellers. "We did not have a single taker on that trip," recalls George. "Not one person booked."

ABOVE
*Richard Meech
throws a picnic
on the first adult
biking trip*

LEFT
*The newspaper
ad that really got
B&R rolling*

George was reluctant to try the idea again. Personally he loved the notion of two-wheel touring for adults but didn't see how it could fly as a business. Richard insisted it was worth another try – what he had in mind was something radically different. Adults on bikes, yes, but with a whole lot of luxury thrown in to soften the adventure. "George wasn't sure these adult bicycling trips were a good idea," Richard recalls, "but he smelled my enthusiasm. Slowly he warmed to the suggestion and agreed to advance me $1,500 for market research."

Richard left George's office, called the *Globe and Mail*, and placed a 2-by-3-inch black and white advertisement for a trip to Burgundy that September. Two weeks later the trip was sold out: twenty-five people had signed up, happily agreeing to pay $1,690 each for an eight-day journey that including airfare, hotels, most meals, and bicycle rental. The market research was compelling. "We were gleeful," remembers Martha, "but we had no idea this venture would become our trajectory."

As the guide on the trip, Richard could see the idea had struck a chord. The travellers were ecstatic – cheerily cycling in the rain, picnicking by the roadside, skinny-dipping in the Canal de Bourgogne, and, in the words of one thirsty participant, drinking *astronomiques* quantities of wine. B&R's innovative formula of combining not-too-strenuous exercise with eighteenth-century

The trip tapped into the current obsession with fitness, fun, and culture, and that was really what these tours were all about

château comfort had introduced a new way for adults to travel – a fresh way to experience and connect with a place. The trip tapped into the current obsession with fitness, fun, and culture, and that, Richard explained, "was really what these tours were all about."

At the end of the trip, when the travellers asked Richard where B&R was going the following summer, he was quick to reply and had more than a few ideas up his sleeve. B&R had been running student trips all over Europe for years and had the know-how and the local contacts to pull together dozens of well-crafted itineraries, each a week-long expansion of a day or two borrowed from the student journey. For the summer of 1981 they offered three adult bicycling trips. Again, they filled in a hurry.

More destinations were added, and in 1982 B&R operated seven adult bicycling trips. Word-of-mouth recommendations spread quickly around Toronto and across Canada, and, occasionally, south of the border too. As the point man for the adult trips, Richard was getting swamped: "I had to plan all the itineraries, do all the marketing and the staffing, and lead at least one trip," he said, yet he saw himself as an ideas person, not a marketing guy. So he turned to his friend Tom Hamilton. Richard had met Tom in the spring of 1981, when he was looking for guides for the upcoming season. Tom spoke some French, enjoyed biking, and had been to Europe once. Perfect, thought Richard, and asked Tom if he wanted to guide an adult bike trip in France that summer. "Sure," he replied – and he loved the experience. Everyone in the group loved Tom too, mainly because he was gregarious and very funny.

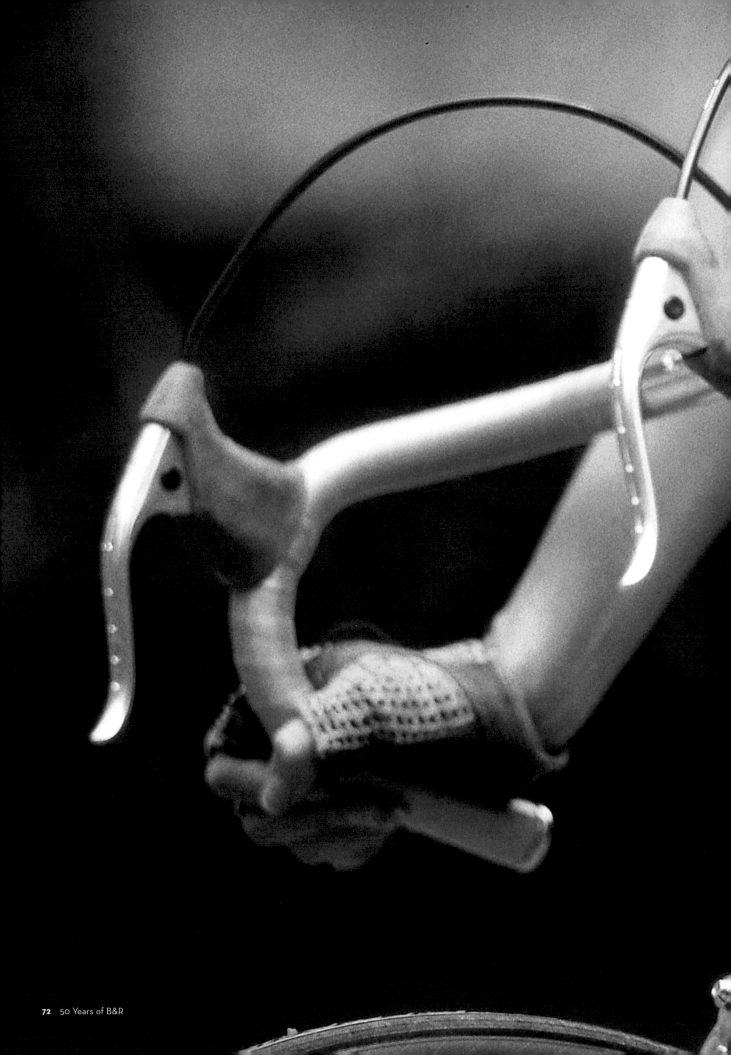

BELOW
*Have bike, will
travel*

RIGHT
*Martha gets the
gang on board
for an AGO trip*

By the fall of 1982 George had decided it was time for B&R to hire someone to focus on marketing, for both the student and the adult programs. Richard suggested he meet with Tom, who had great entrepreneurial drive and was willing to leave his job as a lawyer at Stikeman Elliott. George and Tom got along famously – kindred characters who immediately appreciated each other's charisma and enthusiasm. George offered Tom the position of director of marketing. Although B&R was still a small company with few full-time employees, Tom jumped at the opportunity. "He had no marketing background whatsoever," says Richard. "I think George is a very good judge of character for the people he needs at the time. I don't think it's a science on his part – it's a gut-level response."

Tom was full of ideas about how to grow B&R – in particular, the adult biking portion of the business. One of his first moves was to get some press for the popular new trips. He contacted the *Christian Science Monitor* and convinced the venerable news organization to send a reporter to join a cycling trip through the vineyards of Burgundy. The resulting article, published in April 1983, provided a jovial account of the joys of exploring France B&R style. It was also a journalistic coup in its remarkable avoidance of the word *wine* in describing a ten-day trip through a region renowned for its Pinot Noir and Chardonnay.

Although happy to see the adult biking trips doing so well, George wasn't initially convinced they held much long-term potential. He expressed his reservations in a note to Tom in February 1983: "I know you're concentrating here almost exclusively, but do you think this is wise? I don't know. Personally, I think it's a fun

endeavour. But a *very* limited market. It's your decision, but of course, you need to be right." Notwithstanding his skepticism, George was prepared to give Tom some rope and let him run with it.

Meanwhile, George scanned the horizon in search of bigger markets and signed deals for B&R to represent Abercrombie & Kent in Canada and Sun Line Cruises worldwide. The numbers were tantalizingly large, but George found it frustrating to be held accountable for the quality of another company's trips. As he said, "In a sense, once you represent someone, you are also responsible for the execution of their trips, but there's very little you can do about it."

By contrast, B&R continued to maintain a high degree of control over the trips they created and operated for the AGO and the ROM, and throughout the early eighties both programs flourished. Year after year they came up with evocative, educational adventures for members of both institutions – The Great Whales of Newfoundland, People of the Raven (West Coast Indians & Wildlife), Mughals & Maharajas, Follow Van Gogh to Amsterdam, A Melanesian Adventure, A Photographic Safari in Kenya, and, for explorers of the occult, Haitian Voodoo.

Most exciting for George and Martha were the cruises they operated for the AGO and the ROM. The popularity and financial success of the Follow Ulysses cruise in 1976 inspired B&R to develop a series of similar ship-based trips. For four years, starting in 1980, Martha

spearheaded the research, marketing, and guiding of an elegant Mediterranean cruise, each with its own focus: Lost Cities by the Sea, the Isles of Greece, Ancient Shores, and other stirring themes. It took a huge financial commitment to charter the ship: before B&R could make a profit, they had to reach 70 percent occupancy, despite the recession-riddled Canadian economy at the time. Yet Martha always seemed to reach the target. Along with mothering her two young children, she was also running a separate business of her own – Button Designs – which designed and fabricated Plexiglass furniture and accessories. Her customers included Yul Brynner and the king of Norway.

As enjoyable and profitable as the institutional trips were for the company, George and Martha had a sense that running trips for the AGO and the ROM wasn't an ideal future. There were cost sensitivities to consider and committees to appease. Ultimately, someone else was calling the shots. What B&R really wanted was to be independent – to create its own trips, to build its own brand. Bit by bit, from the mid-eighties onward, the tide of institutional trips started to ebb.

Fortunately, B&R was set to catch another, much bigger wave. Richard and Tom's hunch was right – the future was on a bicycle. In 1983 B&R operated twice as many adult bike trips as the year before. The numbers more than doubled in 1984, and jumped dramaticaly again in 1985. They had grown from a single adult cycling trip in 1980 to seventy-five trips just five years later. Without any conscious goal, B&R had invented exactly the sort of experience the world was looking for – active luxury travel. John Ralston Saul, a pre-eminent Canadian author and long-time friend of George and Martha, likens the B&R approach to a revival of eighteenth- and nineteenth-century travel: "It was really the reinvention of how people can be together – something that once was common but had been lost," he said. "It's the idea that you belong to a society, you want to be with other people, and you want to do something physical and cultural."

Quite apart from fortuitous timing, B&R's rampant success with adult biking trips and, after 1984, with walking trips too was due in large part to Tom's remarkable talent for marketing in myriad persuasive and unorthodox ways. He was especially talented in wooing the media and spent lavish sums hosting extravagant

Without any conscious goal, B&R had invented exactly the sort of experience the world was looking for–active luxury travel

....
PREVIOUS
Rolling solo in the south of France

LEFT
Walkers getting high on life in the Alps

BOTTOM
A pannier pinching a loaf

lunches in New York. The winning formula was simple. He'd book a table at one of the city's hottest restaurants, invite a handful of top editors, regale them with stories of cycling the country roads of Europe, and, just before letting them return half-corked to the office, would murmur regretfully, "I know you're all busy and need to get back to work… but we're about to open a bottle of 1967 Château d'Yquem…" Few returned to their desks, and many developed a close friendship with Tom – and, by extension, B&R.

Tom was also fearless. "He would phone up the head of *Vogue* and offer an all-expenses-paid B&R trip to Burgundy for their best travel writer," recalls Richard. "People do stuff like that all the time now, but they didn't back then. He knew how to get publicity without paying for it." With the American media loving B&R and the U.S. economy steadily growing, bookings from south of the border surged. B&R had found its groove.

After so many years of incremental hard-won growth, it was exhilarating to see the success of the adult biking and walking trips. "When this thing struck, man oh man, did it ever feel good," remembers George. "The numbers were just charging along, and I was thinking at some point we'll rein it in. But right now while it's running, we'll just let her go. Let's go full blast because people are going to see what we're doing, and before long there'll be a lot of competition." For the time being, however, the road was wide open. B&R put its foot to the floor and stomped on the accelerator.

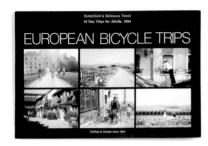

But how to deliver the goods? For the first few years the logistical demands were modest, and there was no need to have a European headquarters. Trip planning and guide hiring were handled from the Toronto office, and B&R's small fleet of bicycles was stored at a bike shop in Paris, La Maison du Vélo, owned by Francis Kelsall, a man *Le Monde* once described as "the Englishman who dares to sell bikes to the French." He was a wonderful guy, doing his best to coordinate the comings and goings of so many bicycles, but the pace of growth began to overwhelm him. Peter Chittick, who had been guiding student trips for B&R since 1980 and had recently moved to Paris to oversee operations for the upcoming season, remembers another complication: "We learned that Francis was having a *contrôle fiscal* (tax audit). He was so disorganized that we worried we would find all our bikes locked up by the French government."

It was time for B&R to find a European home of its own. George gravitated toward Burgundy, a region B&R had been cycling through for almost twenty years. It was central for virtually all of B&R's trips (most of them still in Europe and in France in particular), soaked with history and culture, and exceedingly pretty. On a June day in 1985, George, Tom, and Peter hopped on a train destined for Beaune – the wine capital of Burgundy, just two and a half hours southeast of Paris. Arriving in time for lunch, they found an outdoor table overlooking the Place Carnot in the heart of Beaune, ordered a bottle of impeccably chilled Meursault (from the nearby town of the same name), and settled into their chairs. Neither too big nor too small, this little place would do just fine they agreed.

Beaune Mon Amour

It's easy to fall in love with Beaune. Even in France, with its abundance of beguiling towns, Beaune is a standout. Perfectly formed, well bred, and subtly vivacious, it has mastered the art of eating, drinking, and living well.

For B&R, Beaune has become the physical embodiment of a perfect spiritual partner. It all began innocently enough – an attractive and convenient place to base a business. But the relationship developed quickly. B&R staff working in Beaune for the season needed places to live, so they found apartments and signed leases. Wine was poured, cheeses were served, they got to know the landlord's family, friendships were formed, one thing led to another... *et voilà, l'amour.* "You'd have relationships, you'd have marriages, and it became a rich tapestry of not just being interlopers," says Clare Watlington, "but really being accepted into the fabric."

At least a few dozen semi-nomads from the clan of B&R have settled permanently in Beaune over the years,

After a light meal, they set out to find a space to rent. George walked clockwise around Place Carnot while Tom and Peter walked counterclockwise, confident that one or the other of them would run into a real estate agent. And they did – an enthusiastic local by the name of Pierre-Henri Weiss (whose daughter, Eugénie, currently works with B&R in Beaune). They explained their situation to him and, after a moment's reflection, he gestured wildly and exclaimed, "J'ai une idée!" There was a vast and vacant warehouse on Rue de Seurre, he said, a short walk from the centre of town. By five o'clock that afternoon the lease was signed. Next day they picked up the bikes from Francis's shop in Paris and trucked them down to Beaune.

B&R's active luxury trips were treading fresh ground and had no established path to follow, no pattern to emulate. While everyone working for the company knew exactly what they were there to do – plan and operate the best trips possible – it wasn't always clear *how* to do it. Improvisation was the order of the day, and staff and guides were chosen for their ability to work hard and figure things out along the way. B&R was fostering an environment where attitude and optimism, enthusiasm and experimentation were prized above all else. A somewhat ambiguous note at the bottom of the route instructions given to all the bikers and walkers in the early years sums up the spirit nicely: "There's no such thing as getting lost."

Active luxury trips were a new experience for the hotels and restaurants too. In the spring of 1983 George remembers visiting an elegant chateau in the Loire Valley where he was hoping to book including David Butterfield, George and Martha's son. He walked into Pickwick's Pub (a B&R haunt of considerable repute) for a pint one evening many years ago and caught the eye of a beautiful Beaunoise oenologist named Juliette Lardière. He stayed on, decided to become a wine maker, married Juliette – and they continue to live in Beaune with their three children.

Hundreds more have experienced and enjoyed the pleasures of Beaune on a fleeting basis – guides congregating at the Grand Café for a *bière pression* on their way to their destinations, travellers rolling in for a night or two at Hôtel Le Cep, and staff from the Toronto office finding any excuse to spend a week at the French office.

None of this should imply that Beaune is easy to access. Even pronouncing the name is a challenge if you didn't grow up singing *La Marseillaise*. Somehow the vowels like to be stretched, then kissed with a pucker. The *périphérique*, the ring road that coddles the historic centre, introduces another obstacle. A steady stream of cars whizzing one way around and around again acts like a disorientation field and seems to ask, "Are you sure you're allowed in?"

If you show Beaune the love and respect it deserves, it will love you right back. George and Martha learned that years ago. In 1990 they consummated their romance with the town by having Butterfield & Robinson purchase a derelict but pedigreed three-room stone house known as the Bastion Ste. Anne. Built into the 17th-century rampart wall that surrounds Beaune, the Bastion, a classified historic French monument now beautifully restored (with the help of architect and long-time friend Jack Diamond), is a secret paradise – a vast private garden of pebbled walkways, fruit trees, and quiet places to look up at the clouds. There is even a small stone sentry tower, an *échaugette*, where guards kept watch over the fabled town many metres below. Normally a property of such significance would never be offered for sale to a non-local. But the people of Beaune understand that love is a two-way street, and they know that Butterfield & Robinson is there to stay.

some rooms for an upcoming bike trip. He sat down with the bemused manager, who explained: "Monsieur Butterfield, people arrive at this hotel by Mercedes-Benz, not by bicycle." Before B&R started rolling and strolling through the European countryside, no one ever showed up at a fancy restaurant in a t-shirt and shorts. Yet the reception for the sweaty and smiling B&R travellers was almost always warm and friendly. Their energy and enthusiasm were a breath of fresh air, a playful change of attitude. As the practical maitre d' at a Michelin-starred restaurant once told George, "You can dress in anything you want when you come here. As long as you appreciate the food, we don't care."

It didn't hurt that Butterfield & Robinson was becoming an increasingly significant customer. Year after year the number of trips and travellers continued to balloon. By 1989 more than 4,000 people were signing up annually to participate in B&R's adult biking and walking trips throughout Europe. With twenty-nine distinct itineraries on offer in nearly a dozen countries, the trip-planning machine kept pace by expanding in size and complexity. The Beaune office moved, for a third time, to an even larger property at 5, rue de Cîteaux (B&R's European home base to this day) to accommodate the fleet of more than 1,200 custom-made KHS bicycles, while a team of ten bike mechanics and five route managers worked flat out to feed the voracious operational appetite of the growing business. "We worked seven days a week, all the hours that we could – and we loved it," says Clare Watlington, director of European operations at the time.

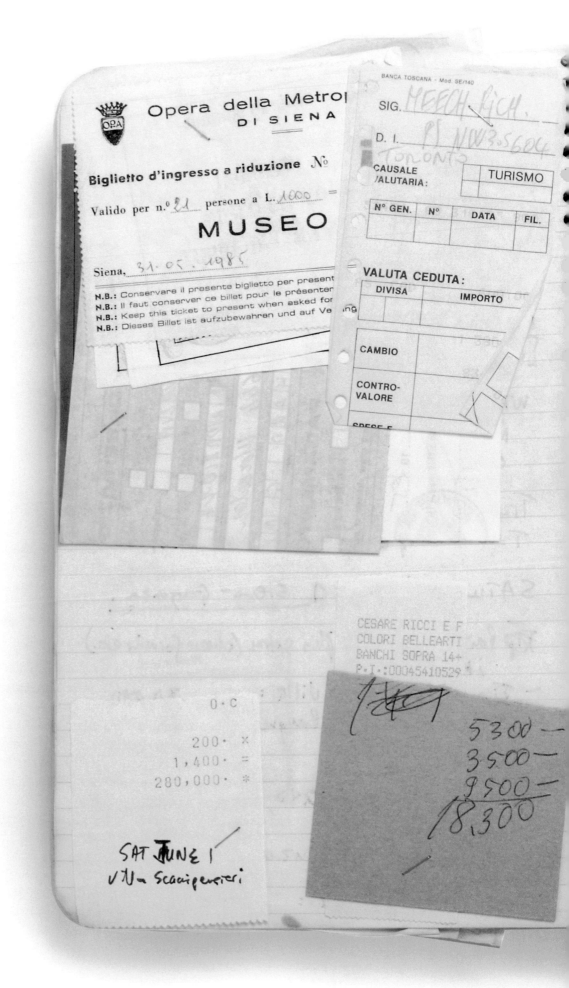

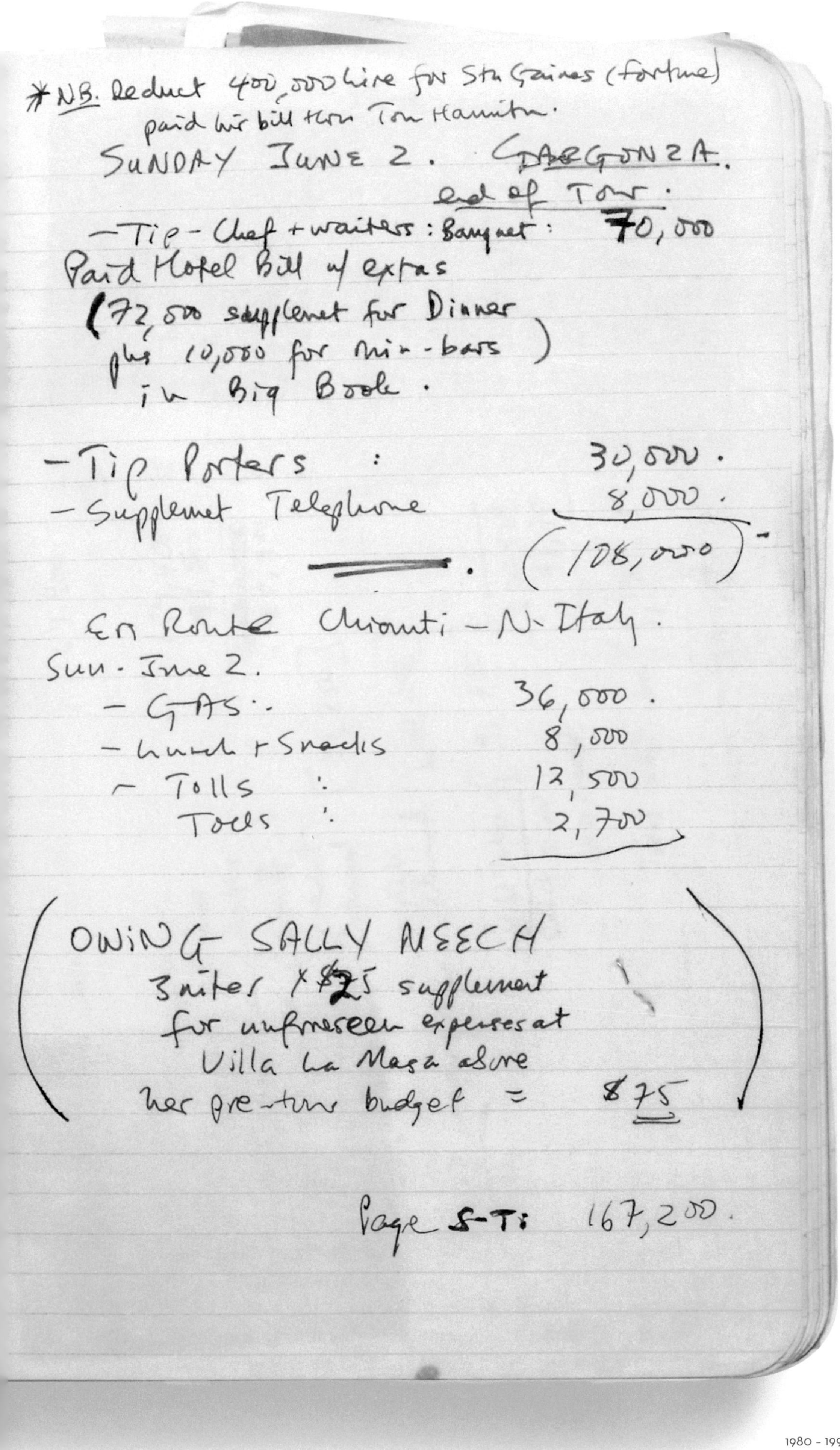

※ NB. Deduct 400,000 lire for Stu Gaines (fortune)
     paid his bill thru Tom Hamilton.

SUNDAY JUNE 2.   GARGONZA.
                        end of Tour.

—Tip - Chef + waiters : Banquet :   70,000
Paid Hotel Bill w/ extras
  (72,000 supplement for Dinner
   plus 10,000 for min-bars)
   in Big Book.

—Tip Porters   :   30,000.
—Supplement Telephone   8,000.
                        ─────────────
                        (108,000)‾

   En Route Chianti — N. Italy.
Sun. June 2.
   — GAS ·   36,000.
   — Lunch + Snacks   8,000
   — Tolls :   12,500
     Tolls :   2,700

(OWING SALLY NEECH
   3 nites X $25 supplement
   for unforeseen expenses at
     Villa La Masa above
   her pre-tour budget = $75)

        Page S-T: 167,200.

Adult biking and walking trips in Western Europe (predominantly in France and Italy) had become B&R's bread and butter, accounting for more than 80 percent of overall revenue. "The numbers were there," says George, "the letters were flowing in, and people were having a great time. It was ecstasy after ecstasy." And because operations seemed to be staying more or less on track, George was free to keep doing what he had always done best – focus on creativity and dream up new trip ideas. Motivated by the fact that there was such an appetite for active luxury travel, B&R tried applying this approach in different ways and places. Horseback riding in Provence and cross-country skiing in Bavaria didn't get much traction, but exotic journeys to China, Bali, Tanzania, and New Zealand definitely struck a chord – and proved that biking and walking was an ideal way to experience almost any destination, not just Europe.

Gil Roberts and his wife, Penny Cohen, signed up for one of the inaugural bike trips to China in 1989 – the first of twenty trips they would take with B&R over the next couple of decades. "We were there while a lot of protests were happening," remembers Gil, "but we never had the sense the hammer was about to fall. On our way home after the trip we had a layover in Vancouver. I turned on the

"We absolutely trusted B&R to provide a great experience. And they did"

TV in our hotel room and saw tanks rolling across Tiananmen Square, where we'd been biking just a week before." Like legions of other hard-working, time-starved, exercise-and-culture craving North Americans, Gil and Penny were sold on the merits of slowing down to see the world: "We absolutely trusted B&R to provide a great experience. And they did."

Political shifts elsewhere on the map were spurring other trip ideas. In the late summer of 1989 Lech Walesa's Solidarity movement outpowered one-party rule in Poland, and it was clear that Communism was faltering in neighbouring countries too. George and Martha sensed an opportunity – a chance once again to be on the creative cutting edge of travel. They picked up the phone and called a young guide, Erik Blachford, who'd first travelled with B&R on a student trip in 1984 and returned a few years later to excel as a trip leader. "I was back in Montreal working for a theatre company when George rang and said he wanted to open up something in Eastern Europe very quickly," Erik recalls. "He needed someone to drop everything, go there for a couple of months, and figure out where we should travel and how we should do it. I told him I didn't speak German or Polish or Czech, so I wasn't his guy. 'No,' he replied, 'you'll be fine.'"

Butterfield & Robinson

1989

Biking and Walking in Europe
for adults · students · families

The following week Erik was on a plane to Poland to have a look around. Beginning in Warsaw, he made his way by bicycle to Krakow, then over to Prague, and eventually up through East Germany. By the time he reached Berlin he sensed that the Wall was about to fall. He pumped coins into a payphone and made an urgent overseas call to George and Martha. They flew to Berlin the very next day to meet with him and walked to the border, which had opened just hours before. "We climbed to the top of an abandoned watch tower overlooking the Wall," remembers Martha. "There were empty vodka bottles all over the floor, but not a guard in site. The scene was so fresh you could still smell the alcohol. We must have been the first people up that tower after the collapse of the Wall."

Later that evening, the three went out for dinner at a small restaurant in East Berlin. When they asked for the bill at the end of the meal the owner came over, shrugged his shoulders, and said, "We don't know what to charge you. I have no idea what our currency is worth – pay me what you think is fair." They paid three times the price of the meal according to the menu and continued into the night.

ABOVE
David Borins and Nathalie Butterfield take a break on a bike trip in France

The villages and countryside weren't yet ready for B&R prime time, so Erik and Martha decided instead to create an urban walking trip. She returned twice the following year to do more research and guide the inaugural trip.

Digging deep into the history and culture of a destination was always a top priority when creating new trips – partly because it made for a more memorable and fun experience but also because B&R wanted its travellers to learn something. Throughout the eighties, Student World, as the student program was called, pioneered a number of innovative academic programs. There were opportunities to study art in Siena or Cambridge, Italian in Rome, or French in one of three European locales (Bayonne, Nice, Switzerland). For students hoping to pick up some French while working on their backhand, B&R offered Matchpoint, a tennis camp in Quebec.

Sally Meech (Richard's younger sister and one of five siblings who all guided for B&R) shepherded the student program from 1983 to 1990. She knows what a huge and positive impact the trips had on the kids: "It gave them a wonderful balance in responsibility and direction," she says. "An extraordinary camaraderie developed among the students because only if you had shared that experience could you realize how special it was." Unfortunately, changing times and attitudes meant that fewer students were looking for a chaperoned travel experience. Young people had more freedom, and they wanted to explore on their own and backpack. The

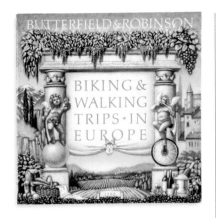

student program was losing momentum. The opposite was true with the adult biking and walking trips.

"The horses were running and they were just going wild," remembers George with a slow shake of his head. The media, which Tom had whipped into a frenzy, could barely produce articles on the trips fast enough. On one occasion an editor at *Gourmet* magazine called Tom and offered to write a feature on B&R if he'd agree to join her for dinner at Le Crocodile, a restaurant in Strasbourg that had just received a coveted third Michelin star. Tom wanted a twelve-page article for the effort, but settled for ten pages. Meanwhile the travellers were competing to sign up for trips. The operational machine was starting to creak and groan under the weight of success.

Martha, who was still guiding regularly, recalls a conversation with a traveller ("a business guru from Boston") who expressed concern at the exponential growth rate: "He told me it wasn't safe to grow more than 15 percent a year. We would not be able to keep up operationally, he warned, and we'd kill ourselves. But none of us paid any attention. We didn't have rules about anything." Richard agrees: "It was a little chaotic. Things did get a little frayed at times."

B&R was caught in a whirlwind of sensational growth, and it was a constant challenge keeping operations on track. Part of the issue was a singular obsession with the on-trip experience. "I remember people saying that the only thing George cared about was that everybody should have a great time on these trips," recalls Erik. "So long as that happened, you never got into any trouble. It's a funny thing to say, but it didn't feel like a business. It felt more like every day you were working in the arts – putting on a show." Travellers were loving the performance, which was critical and the very reason sales were so robust. But behind the curtain, other areas of the business were not getting the day-to-day attention they needed.

....
BELOW
*Elated students
fresh from a jump
in the fountain*

Lucky Break
Vicky Bake

Sometimes it's incredibly convenient when people do *not* answer the phone. On a muggy summer morning in 1989 George sat at his desk, quietly contemplating a call he was about to make to Jennifer Cramer, an editor at *Town & Country* magazine. He wanted to explain to her that the Spanish biking trip he had enthusiastically offered to plan for one of the magazine's writers and a small group of friends was not going to happen. After three weeks of searching within B&R, he hadn't been able to find anyone who knew Spain well enough to pull a trip together.

But Jennifer wasn't at her desk, so George left a brief message asking her to call him back.

Thinking he'd clear his head with a walk around the block, he made his way to the door, pausing for a moment to lean into the office of Nicky Speakman, the guide coordinator, to let her know he was giving up the search for a Spain expert. By chance, Vicky Bake, the twenty-two-year-old interviewee sitting across from Nicky, had lived in Spain for several months during high school and spoke the language

fluently. "I chatted with George a little bit," says Vicky, "and the next thing you know we had a map on the table and he starts pointing out a hotel here and a hotel there. Then he asked me if I could make a few phone calls, because this was July and the trip was going to run in September."

When Jennifer returned George's call later that afternoon, he knew exactly what to say. "The trip is coming together beautifully," he assured her. "We've lined up a fantastic woman who knows Spain well to lead the tour."

Two days later, Vicky was on a plane to Europe. Realizing she had never guided a trip, much less researched and planned one from scratch, George sent her on a biking trip to Alsace so she could experience first hand as a traveller what a B&R trip was all about. Then she went on to Spain for three weeks of research. And so B&R's initial biking trip to Spain came together.

A guide's first trip is overwhelming at the best of times, but for Vicky there was an added variable. Both George and Sidney were there. "It was all a bit challenging," she confides, "especially the day we lost Sidney. I thought I might lose my job." After a luxuriously long lunch, most of the bikers went one way with George, but Sidney decided to try a different route. Vicky was driving the support van, and when she arrived at the village where they had arranged to watch a bullfight, she couldn't find Sidney anywhere. Perhaps in the flurry of it all, she thought, she might even have driven him off the road. When George heard that Sidney was missing, the euphoria quickly drained from his afternoon. He got into the van with Vicky and went looking. Before long they found him – following one of B&R's well-understood principles, "There's no such thing as getting lost," he took a few unscheduled turns and ended up having a nap in a cool vineyard.

For the next fifteen years Vicky worked full time for B&R – a trusted leader at the helm of the Beaune office.

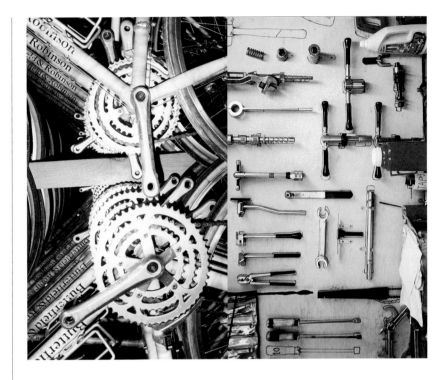

George started to follow another hunch. Maybe it was time to bring in someone to help get things under control. Tom suggested that he meet with Danny Legault, an old friend from Queen's University. Like George (and Tom, Peter, and countless B&R guides before and since), Danny had trained as a lawyer – de facto evidence for George that he was smart, hard-working, and not afraid. His work background was also intriguing. After finishing law school, Danny had joined the Royal Canadian Air Force and become a jet fighter pilot, a sign that he might have an aptitude for structure, process, and leadership. Still, the conversation danced along for four weeks. "I wanted to get to know George, and he wanted to get to know me," says Danny.

In the late spring of 1989 Danny joined B&R as vice-president of operations and immediately flew to France – a reconnaissance mission to Beaune. What he found when he walked into the office was unlike anything he'd experienced in the military. There was no obvious chain of command and minimal paper work to support the considerable flow of cash and cheques to guides and suppliers. The swelling fleet of bikes and gear was like an enormous snowball rolling down the side of a mountain. Amazingly, a mild-mannered mid-twenties Canadian, Geoff Sandquist, who'd been hired as a bike mechanic the summer before and had recently assumed responsibility for B&R's entire technical operation, was capably coordinating the movement of hundreds of bikes to and from trips all over Europe every week. The homegrown system was working, but ripe for refinement.

For a cost of $25,000, Danny ordered two gigantic magnetic boards and had them installed on the office wall in Beaune. After tiny coloured

magnetic strips were arranged in the grid pattern, they formed a primitive yet reliable way to keep track of the swirl of trips, guides, bikes, and vans. The accounting department gasped in disbelief when they got the invoice, but George supported the purchase. "He was so great that way," recalls Danny. (To this day the magnetic boards are still in use, so it was a worthwhile expenditure after all.)

Another simple remedy introduced to ease communication was a morning meeting, known as Huddle, held every day at 9 sharp in both the Toronto and the Beaune offices. More than being an effective tool for sharing information in the pre-Internet era, it proved a wonderful way to nurture B&R's playful culture. There staff celebrated birthdays and sales milestones with equal vigour, shared entertaining highlights from trips on the road, and enjoyed enormous wheels of Parmesan. Huddle ensured that the day started off on the right foot – and on time.

One of Danny's more elaborate innovations was a spiralling concrete ramp leading from the first to the second floor of the Beaune office. The theory was that staff and guides could ride their bikes up and down, between the floors, saving time while having some fun. In practice, however, the pitch of the ramp proved too steep to safely ride. It was eventually removed at twice the cost of initial construction.

Determined to bring structure and efficiency to B&R's operations, Danny ultimately turned to his greatest love – technology. After implementing a customer relationship management system – to streamline and individualize B&R's marketing efforts – he hired a group of software developers to build a custom reservation system. Affectionately nicknamed Picard (after Captain Jean-Luc Picard from the television series *Star Trek*), the system was intolerably buggy and proved a challenge to integrate with the company's existing software. "Danny was so smart," says Martha, "but we didn't always understand what he was talking about. Nobody had much concept of what information technology was back then."

Much more intuitive for most of the staff was fun management. And with B&R booming beyond belief and money flooding into the business, there were many lavish celebrations. In Beaune, parties seemed to happen spontaneously almost every night. Bike mechanics, route managers, and logistics coordinators needing to blow off steam would rendezvous around a courtyard table to share a laugh, break bread, inhale wonderfully stinky local cheeses, and raise a glass of divine Burgundian wine. Or they'd meet up with guides at local bars and restaurants to hear fresh-from-trip stories about the traveller who got lost for hours after reading his map upside down or the woman who wore her bike helmet backwards for the entire trip. "Everyone was always in a good mood," Clare remembers. "Everyone was beautiful and fun and happy and spending money."

RIGHT
*Les mecs
keeping it cool*

BELOW RIGHT
*Slip and a dip in
southern France*

The good times always came to a crescendo at the end-of-season gathering held each year in late October near Beaune or some other colourful destination in Europe. On the tail of the busiest and most successful season anyone at B&R had ever experienced, the party marking the end of the 1990 season was particularly memorable. More than seventy-five guides and full-time staff made their way to southern France to spend the weekend at Crillon le Brave, a charming and luxurious hotel that Peter Chittick (who'd left B&R a few years earlier) and a group of investors had shaped out of a classic Provencal hill town. The ebullient crowd, lavishly dressed in Halloween costumes, gathered around the outdoor pool and grew more rambunctious with each apéritif. By the time dinner was ready to be served, the tables had been cleared and rearranged to form a long platform.

At that point Peter grabbed a microphone and introduced his hotel staff members. They then walked down the makeshift runway like fashion models, hamming it up for the audience. Finally, a timid and terrified dishwasher shuffled down the tables while some of the women ripped off their shirts and threw them at him. "For three hours it was like a nuclear explosion," recalls Danny. "I remember pouring a half-bottle of cognac on Tom's head and lighting it with a match. POOF! The flames went up in a fireball." Remarkably, Tom was not injured by the incident. In some respects the party was a reflection of the times – the decade of decadence that was the eighties. But more than that the exuberant behaviour was a Dionysian display of the ecstatic energy that erupts when like-minded souls gather to celebrate a shared experience.

And then the hangover set in – big time.

While B&R had been enjoying a biking bacchanalia in Europe, Saddam Hussein and the Iraqi army were walking into Kuwait. Through the late summer and fall of 1990, coalition forces began arriving in the region as tensions rose. On January 17, 1991, the United States unleashed Operation Desert Storm, and for the next six weeks the conflict raged while the entire world watched to see what would happen next.

At the B&R office on Bond Street in Toronto, the telephones were silent. Sales, which had been robust through the autumn, went down to nothing. The timing could hardly have been worse. January was the start of B&R's most crucial booking season, a four-month window during which 75 percent of the total trip reservations for the year were made. Danny remembers spending twelve hours punching numbers into an elaborate series of linked spreadsheets he'd developed, only to arrive at a stark and terrifying bottom line. "Holy %&#@, we're going to lose millions of dollars," he told George and Tom.

Since 1966 Butterfield & Robinson had been merrily following a vision, tenaciously trying this and that, blazing a trail. Even when things were challenging, the company continued to call its own shots. But now, according to Geoff Sandquist, they "saw for the first time the frailties of the travel industry and how it can be affected by things we cannot control." In the six weeks after the start of Operation Desert Storm, B&R let go of twenty-four people – almost half the full-time staff. It was a discombobulating and heart-wrenching period.

Much to everyone's surprise, the phones soon started ringing again. The Gulf War came to an official close on February 28, 1991, and by May booking patterns were back to a normal pace. B&R finished the year with roughly 40 percent fewer travellers than the year before, but it was still in business. Equally important, the company was lean, alert, and ready to evolve. It was time for a new strategy.

As on his first day on the job, Tom remained convinced that adult biking trips in Europe were the future for B&R. More than that, he wanted to expand the offering to include group corporate travel and self-guided bike trips. He insisted that B&R's global operation should be run out of France. In late 1991 he and his wife, Athlyn Fitz-James (who had been working at B&R for close to a decade and was instrumental in the birth and growth of the walking trips),

decided to move to France and work out of B&R's Beaune office. Issues with the new arrangement soon appeared. The role that Tom had created for himself demanded a high degree of administrative and operational input (also known as office-based grunt work), which was not something he loved. At the same time, he had distanced himself from the thing he was best at – marketing. With the brochures being produced in Toronto, virtually all of B&R's travellers based in North America, and Tom living in a French town thousands of miles away, the new set-up didn't make a lot of sense – at least not for B&R.

Meanwhile, Danny was back in the Toronto office trying hard to pull B&R into the future and whip the numbers into shape. In the fall of 1992 he was promoted to president. George's goal was to remain the creative force behind the company while Danny focused on operations. All the years that George had been building Butterfield & Robinson, he'd also been rapidly growing another business – Butterfield & Company, the Bermuda-based food importing business he and his brother, Jim Butterfield, had purchased from their father in 1981. Driving the two businesses simultaneously was demanding, and George hoped that Danny's promotion would ease his own involvement in B&R's daily management.

It didn't play out that way. In a matter of months, George couldn't help but step back into the ring. Too many software and reservation system initiatives were being chased, he felt, and not enough attention paid to follow-through. Things were unnecessarily

ABOVE
A long and winding road in Piemonte, Italy

RIGHT
A button broadcasting George's sales forecast for 1992 (he was off by five people)

GEORGE'S GUT FEEL 3645

complicated, priorities were out of whack, and fundamentals were being ignored. "Too little common sense and too much new-fangled jargon isn't going to get us very far," wrote George in a memo in the spring of 1993. He wanted to refocus B&R on three core activities: planning trips, selling trips, and operating trips. And not just any trips. "We are not striving to be the biggest, only the best," read the last line of the memo.

Something else was shifting in George – a realization that B&R could be more than a great company. It had potential, he knew, to be a terrific business. "Up to that time," recounts Paul Christopher, the accountant Danny hired in 1992, "B&R could not make money two years straight. Even when it had dynamite years, there was nothing on the bottom line. The profit was all frittered away, and there were leaks in the bucket all over the place." When the end-of-year accounting fog cleared in the spring of 1993, however, B&R discovered that it had made a record profit on the trips it ran in 1992. The new accounting department had developed detailed trip budgets for the first time. Finally, costs were getting under control.

The little travel company that George, Martha, and Sidney had started on a whim twenty-seven years before was coming of age.

Alpha
Guides

It takes a special breed of person to guide biking and walking trips – one part motivational therapist, one part bike mechanic, one part diplomat, one part gastronome, and two parts cheerleader. Every guide is unique and yet they're all cut from the same cloth.

	1 - 2	3 - 4	5 - 6
It all adds up Some guides lead one trip a year, others more than twenty.	**1380** Total guides	**934** Guides	**220** Guides	**100** Guides

A Amina Abdeljawad | Tracey Aberman | Marianne Abraham | Tom Abraham | Line Abrahamian | Eden Abrahams | Mark Abruzzese | Eric Accili | Natalie Adamov | Mike Adams | Rob Adamson
Anderson | Ray Andrews | Steven Andrews | Erica Anthony | Alexa Antonio | Caroline Apffel | Simon Aplin | Lina Appleby | Lynn Appleby | Luis Arevalogarcia | Darius Arjang | Susan Armanini | Jac
Bruce Bailey | Victoria Bake | Ann Baker | Paolo Balduzzi | Ned Baldwin | Kevin Ball | Tony Ball | Matthew Ballantine | Louise Bang | Joe Barbieri | Belinda Bard | Sarah Bardet | Tibor Barna | Sa
Beauroy | Gary Bedell | Fiona Beeston | Marcel Behr | Wivina Belmonte | Nancy Benitz | Andy Benkovitz | Carolyn Bennett | Liane Benoit | Lance Berelowitz | Sabrina Berent | Simon Bergmann | D
Rosemary Bird | Sarah Bird | Patrick Birmingham | Manuela Biron | Marco Biron | Paolo Biron | Erik Blachford | Iris Black | Peter Blackman | Andrea Blaikie | Antony Blaikie | Adrienne Blattel | Hol
Bott | Enrica Boucher | Annik Boulva | Genevieve Boulva | Chris Bovaird | Noelle Bovon | Daniel Bower | Jordan Bower | James Boyd | Ernle Bradford | Mara Bralove | Eirikka Brandson | Robin Bre
Brown | Shona Brown | Leslie Browning | Leslie Bruce | Fred Bruemmer | Theresa Brunner | Kira Bruschke | Anthony Bucci | Barbara Buck | Julia Bunting | Damien Burel | Trent Burgiss | Mike Bur
Cain | Marcela Caldas | Allegra Calder | Andrew Calder | Thane Calder | Susan Callado | Hatha Callis | David Calver | Agustin Calvetti | Dave Camacho | Mark Campbell | Sheila Campbell | Luca C
Sherry Chang | Gordon Charlton | Vicki Charlton | David Charnes | Sarah Chase | Thomas Chase | Alison Cheeseman | Kyl Chhatwal | Peter Chittick | Kyra Chomak | Amrita Choudhury | Sue-Lin
Marcia Cleary | Naomi Clement | Janine Cloney | Ian Cobham | Jillian Cohen | Bill Coleman | Lisanne Collett | David Colucci | Jeff Condry | Jane Connor | Mary Connor | Jeff Conyers | Dani C
Cousens | Celine Cousteau | Lise-Anne Couture | Benson Cowan | David Cox | Carol Coxon | Lauren Craig | Christina Crescenzi | Annie Crisp | Dana Cronin | Tecca Crosby | Jennifer Crouser | T
Dalrymple | Nicolas Danan | Jack Dancy | Gratianne Daum | Caroline Davidson | Ben Davies | Carol Davies | Todd Davis | Maria De Carvalho Lopes | Chris de Koos | Cheryl de Leeuw | Gerry de Lee
Deluca | Sarah DeMott | Lloyd Dennis | Catherine Dent | Anuj Desai | Carmela Di Dio | Jacopo Di Lorenzo | Claudio Di Todaro | Tony DiBella | Alvaro David Diez Diaz | Sandra Diem | Nicholas Dill | Ba
Diana Dopson | Jean-Louis Doss | Kathleen Driscoll | Cindy Drukier | Rob Drummond | Ghislaine du Planty | Celina Ducceschi | Ken Dudley | Christie Dufault | Mark Duffield | Eimear Duggan | John D
Elliott | Tim Elms | Vanessa Emery | Mackenzie Emond | Leif Engberg | Kurt Engebrecht | Thilo Erhardt | Ulrike Erhardt | Annabel Euvrard | Charlotte Evans | Lewis Evans | Yvette Evers | **F** David F
Feldman | Faerthen Felix | Lisa Ferrari | Zeila Ferro | George Ferzoco | Paolo Fietta | Ana Figueroa | Andrea Filippone | Michele Fillion | Laura Finch | Mark Fincham | Aaron Finnegan | Mireille Fiset |
Jonathan Foyle | Sinead Foyle | Mary Frangakis | Alessio Frangioni | Lila Fraser | Morna Fraser | Julianne Frawley | Scott Frederick | Amy Freeman | Andra Freiberg | Jessica Friedberg | Thomas F
Gambone | Tysen Gannon | Monica Garaitonanda | Florian Garcenot | Megan Gardner | Andy Garner | Marcello Garrisi | Jackie Garrow | Amanda Gary | Shura Gat | Gorana Gavrilov | Kimberly Ga
Glick | Laurie Goldberg | Alina Goldstein | Michael Goldstein | Michele Gonzalez Arroyo | David Gooderham | Christopher Goodwin | Jacqui Goodwin | Chris Gora | Leon Gosney | Ron Gosney | K
Robert Grieve | Peter Griffin | Theresa Griffin | Lori Grossman | Paule Guerin | Shannon Guihan | Stephanie Gulledge | Anne Guthrie | Steve Guttenberg | Kate Guy | **H** Alison Haber | Daniel Haeber
Christine Hanson | Kurt Hanzlik | James Hare | Sara Hare | Ben Harley | Richard Harley | Alan Harman | Barbara Harper | Keith Harris | Jennifer Harrison | Emilie Hartigan | Cameron Harvey | Mic
Saakje Hazenberg | Katie Healy | Richard Heft | Larisa Heimert | Orjan Helland | Harriet Heller | David Henderson | Heather Henderson | Debbie Henley | Christy Herman | Marcey Hess | Kimberly
Erica Holt | Julie Holt | Donald Holzworth | Patricia Homonylo | Georgia Hood | Yuno Hooyuar | John Hornstein | Emily Horton | Mark Horton | Alan Householder | Jason Houston | Daphne Howard
Hunnisett | Marianne Hunt | Megan Hunter | Paul Huschilt | Susan Hutt | Melissa Hyatt | **I** Anita Iaconangelo | Judit Illes | Deanne Inman | Anne Inneo | Luca Innocenti | Joe Iozzo | Yumi Irako | D
Jenkinson | Caroline Jerabek | Pradhat Jha | Karen John | Judy Johnson | Laura Johnson | Chris Jones | Fred Jones | Jenny Jordan | Nathalie Jordi | Andrew Jowett | Val Jurdjevic | **K** Janet Ka
Nicholas Kemplen | Andrew Kennedy | Chuck Kennedy | Nevil Keogh | Richard Keogh | Annette Kerckhoff | Jennifer Kernaghan | Manuela Khoury | Rachel Kimel | Anthony King | Janice Kinney | And
Richard Koegl | Jacquie Koenig | Andreas Kogelnik | Eugene Konitz | Leslie Korrick | Michael Kosaka | Laurie Koshgarian | Kristine Kowalchuk | Don Krsinar | Jeff Krueger | Magda Kryt | Cora Kur
Lane | Noel Langan | Jonathan Lansdell | Kevin Lantz | Dina Lanzi | Marc Lavine | Colleen Law | Jennifer Le Corre | Jeremy Leach | Stephane Leclerc | Patrick Lee | Susannah Lees | Jamie Leese
Lewis | Lisa Lewis | Sarah Lewis | Megan Libby | Jonnel Licari | Bill Liddle | Hilary Lieberman | Emily Lievens | Lisa Liljeberg | Michael Lindstrom | Jennifer Lindström | Brian Linehan | Nicole Lipma
Jennifer Lonergan | Gavin Lord | Ruth Louden | Kasi Lubin | Pascal Lucas | Denis Luccantoni | Patrick Luciani | Ryan Lurie | Paola Lusetti | Luciana Lussu | Lisa Lyons | **M** Veronika Macas | Lisa
MacFarlane | Iain MacInnis | Gillian MacKay | Gwen Mackay-Smith | Lisa Mackay-Smith | Sandy Mackay-Smith | Brad Mackenzie | Sarah MacKenzie | Michael Macklem | Sarah MacLachlan | Karen
Manchur | Carrie Mandel | Laura Manzano Outeiral | Maureen Manion | Ross Manson | Glyn Manwaring-Jones | Paolo Maragliulo | Guillaume Marchant | Rick Marchant | Chris Mark | Meredith Mark
Diego Matamoros | Robyn Matamoros | Tam Mathews | Colleen Mathieu | Jan Matthews | Tam Matthews | Lara Mattioli | Hunter May | Roxana McAllister | Seth McAllister | Joelle McCaffrey | Mich
Kelly McEvenue | Mimi McEvenue | Matthew McEwen | Scott McEwen | Ann McGavin | Jimmy McGavin | Colleen McGrath | D'Arcy McGrath | Ken McGrath | Sarah McHattie | Roberto McKeever
McMeekin | Sarah McNamer | Kiloran McRae | Jessie McVeigh | Nan Meech | Peter Meech | Richard Meech | Sally Meech | Susan Meech | Craig Meier | Ernie Mellegers | Elizabeth Meltz | Kate Me
Mills | Heather Milnes | Kymberly Milroy | Robert Minnes | Tabita Miotto | Mamta Mishra | Nefeli Misuraca | Erik Mitbrodt | Beth Mitchell | Angela Mitchell Sunkur | Sakis Mitsoulis | Sarah Mlezcko |
Morgan | Leslie Morrison | Valeria Morrow | David Morton | Richard Mottram | Mariska Mourik | Fares Moussa | JoAnn Moysey | Val Moysey | Warrick Mueller | Duane Mugford | Russell Muirhead |
Mutterperl | Antoine Muzard | Cynthia Myer | **N** Brett Naisby | Leonard Nalencz | Igor Nardin | Ted Nation | Craig Nattress | Kristin Nedzelski | Donna Neftin | Heather Neill | Michelle Neilson | Hilare
Karen Normandy | Andrea Nottage | Mario Novella | Vladislav Novikov | Riccardo Nucci | Mark Nusca | Toby Nussbaum | **O** Annie O'Brian | Martha O'Brien | Ann O'Connell | Brendan O'Connell | D
Orr | Chat Ortved | Paul Osborne | Jane Osler | Irena Ossola | Brian Osterlin | Marty Ostermiller | Lindsay Owen | **P** Luca Pacchioni | Chris Paddison | Denis Page | Anna Pagliarulo | Gino Palarchio
Pavan | Robert Pearlstein | Kathleen Peggar | Josiane Peltier | Rob Pendergast | Annalise Penfold | Tom Pennacchietti | Barbara Penner | Susan Pepin | Amy Perttula | Christian Petronio | Katja Philip
Anou Pons | Viviane Ponti | Scott Poole | Elio Popolo | Marco Porcellana | Catherine Porter | Dorothy Porter | Lisa Postec | Sean Potts | Rosemary Power | Yvonne Power | Sarah Price | Rafael Pri
Rainey | Joy Ramirez | Caroline Ramsey | Shalmali Rao | Kathryn Rattee | Nigel Ravenhill | Donna Raxlan | Gerda Reeb | Erin Reed | Sue Reed | Christian Rees | David Regan | Derrick Reisky | Jame
Julie Ritchie | Camille Riviere | Gecchi Rizzo | Jules Roazen | Chris Robbins | Therese Roberts | Bruce Roberts | Christian Robertson | Andrea Robinson | Sam Robinson | Sidney Robinson | Mar
Rohmer | Janek Romero | Sebastian Romero | Jim Rooney | Matthew Rose | Andrew Rosenberg | Betsy Ross | Dan Ross | David Ross | Sally Ross | Natalie Roth | Michael Rothschild | Vincenza R
essica Russell | Aimee Russillo | Amanda Russo | Andrea Russo | Joanne Russo | Erik Rutherford | Caitlin Ryan | Mark Ryhorski | Gavin Ryle | Mark Ryle | **S** Agnieszka Sababady | Leon Sachs
Saucier | Shaun Sava | Stefano Scaccia | Olivia Scalliet-Collin | Pinuccia Scatizzi | Emmanuel Scerri | Tim Schellenberger | Henry Schiewind | Don Schmitt | Tim Schoahs | Cindy Schultz | Allison S
Heather Semple | Amy Serafin | Leah Serinsky | Rogerio Seve Marins | Alex Severens | Meera Shanker | Adam Shapero | Johanna Shapira | Valerie Shapley | Lisa Sharvatt | John Sheedy | Megan She
Sinclair | Carolyn Singer | Jennifer Sipple | Kristin Skager | Michael Slinger | Peter Smale | Brad Smith | Darren Smith | Karen Smith | Kevin Smith | Linda Smith | Steve Smith | Suzanne Smith | Ian Sm
Nathalie St Pierre | Stephanie Stanfield | Jennifer Stanley | Jennifer Stanley | Anna Starke | Matthew Starnes | Rebecca Stasko | Robyn Stevan | Helen Stevenson | Michael Stevenson | Anne Stewa
Stoneham | Catherine Streeter | Guido Stucchi | Danielle Stynes | Terry Sullivan | Katerina Summerhays | Mark Summers | Carolyn Sumner | Darryn Sutherland | Jeneen Sutherland | Kate Sutherlar
Erica Taylor | Jill Taylor | Robin Taylor | Ned Teitelbaun | Sonia Ter Hovanessian | Linda Terrier | Nathalie Theillard de Chardin | Sherry Thevenot | Nanci Thomas | Stephanie Thompson | Chris Th
ucker | Michelle Tupko | Shawn Turnau | Michael Turner | Christopher Tweel | **U** Austin Uiska | Basia Ujejski | Tony Urquhart | **V** Virginie Valcauda | Marya Valli | Giorgio Valvassori | Alice Elisabe
Maria Verdicchio | Stéphane Véron-Rainu | Leanna Verrucci | Patrick Vespa | Lidia Vetturetti | Myfanwy Vickers | John Vincent | Sjoerd Vink | Fanny Viret | Mina Volpe | Annette Von Herrmann |
Marianna Waters | Olive Watkins | Matthew Watkins | Clare Watlington | Jennifer Watson | Sue Watson | Amy Watt | Vivian Watt | Kathie Wayne | Melanie Webb | Anthony Weersing | Jennifer Weilan
Sara Whitney | Chris Wieland | Christopher Wieland | Alan Wilkinson | Andrew Wilkinson | Liz Willette | Maclin Williams | Lottie Williams-Burrell | Candy Wilson | Eric Wilson | Michael Wilson | Ross
David Young | Georgia Yuill | Carlos Yuste | **Z** Luciano Zago | Anne Zakula | Auric Zander | Katy Zeidler | Verena Zeigler | Sue Zelinski | David Zemans | Norman Zhang

Sharry Aiken | Neomee Alain | Nicholas Albanese | Scott Alcock | Shannon Alexander | Patrick Allen | Justin Amann | Tony Amaro | Gerardo Amortegui | Kim Anderson | Kim Anderson | Susanne

Megan Armstrong | Shanley Arnett | Tannis Arnett | Gillian Arthur | Phillip Assis | Paul Attwood Philippe | Mikael Aubin | David Avery | Jaime Awe | Leanne Axford | Kendall Ayoub **B** Gina Babbit

Pietro Barrigazzi | Telmo Barros | Michael Basham | Amy Baskerville | Heidi Basset | Adriano Basso | Jacquie Bastick | Rob Baxter | Stacey Beamer | Chris Bean | Stephane Beauroy | Stéphane

Patrick Bermingham | Jessica Bertke | Annie Besse | Giovanni Bettio | Anu Bhalla | Magaly Bianchini | Nat Bichot | Oscar Biedma | Robin Bienenstock | Giorgina Bigioni | Martha Binks | Matt Binnie

ne Blin | Sam Blyth | Elizabeth Boesen | Chris Boivaird | Nina Bombier | Stephanie Bonic | Alberto Bonomi | Adam Borden | Laura Borden | Jerome Bore | Lesley Borggard | Sara Borins | Candace

nton | Lisa Breschi | Paul Brewin | Nick Breyfogle | Tatiana Brisolla | Cindy Broda | Rita Brogley | Lori Broglio | Stephen Broni | John Brooks | Julian Brosch | Craig Brown | Kristen Brown | Philippe

| Joanne Burns | Wendy Burrell | Slate Burris | David Butterfield | Deborah Butterfield | George Butterfield | Martha Butterfield | Nathalie Butterfield | Tom Butterfield **C** John Caccia | Christina

ren Cappell | Bianca Cappellini | Eric Carlson | Françoise Carragher | Sally Carson | Rebecca Cash | Sean Cash | Brian Catlos | Francesca Cestari | Ana Cevallos | Adrian Chalk | Chris Chamber

Churcher Churcher | Roberto Cipolla | Sigrid Claasen | Amie Claps | Michael Clark | Sarah Clark | Hilary Clarke | Madeline Clarke | Kyra Clarkson | Sheila Claudi | Christina Clausen | Karen Clausen

ook | Annabel Cooper | James Cooper | Jane Cooper | Heather Corcoran | Jack Corsello | Terri Corso | Rogelio Corte | Karen Cossar | Tim Costigan | Stella Couban | Nancy Coulter | Elizabeth

da Currie | Shane Curry | Marie-Louise Cusack | Natalie Cutler-Welsh | Christopher Cwynar | Marysia Czarsk **D** Robert d'Arras | Damian D'Cruz | Grace D'Ercole | Alex Dale | Gus Dale | Libby

Mers | Miranda de Pencier | Nick de Pencier | Lisa De Pieri | Maurits de Planque | Gill Deacon | Jennifer Deacon | William Debost | Kimberley Deck | Angelo Del Priori | Sandro Della-Mea | Salvatore

nn Dillon | Tyler Dillon | Martha Dingle | Tam Dinh Ngoc | Andrea Dinnick | Kevin diPirro | Charlotte Disher | Gwen Dobie | Chris Donald | Victoria Donaldson | Catherine Donnell | Siobhan Donoghue

Duskova | Hugh Duthie | Jaime Dutton | Nigel Dyche **E** Jennifer East | Derek Eaton | M.G. Eaton | Michael Ede | Richard Edwards | Tony Egan | Brahm Eiley | Kristi Elborne | Danielle Elkin | Simon

alcon | Amy Falkner | Rosa Falvo | Alex Fandel | Giacomo Fano | Patrick Farges | David Farnell | Kathy Farris | Ellen Farrow | Rachel Faulise | Andrew Fedosov | Julie Fehrle | Marten Fekkes | James

. M. Fisher | Athlyn Fitz-James | Robert Fitzgerald | Gavin Flinn | Kathryn Flynn | Cristina Fogale | Greg Foley | Patrick Ford | Jonathon Fortier | Anne-Michele Fortin | Rachel Foulkes | Leslie Fournier

riesen | Gregor Fuchshuber | Cesare Fuoco | Patti Furlong | Jesse Fyfe **G** Regan Gage | Juan Gali | Erin Gallagher | Paul Gallagher | Benj Gallander | Bernadette Gallez | Deborah Gallin | Guido

Gedye | Betsy Geller | Sylvia Giacon | Orietta Gianjorio | Dick Gibb | Clare Gibbons | Julie Gibson | Kate Gibson | Jim Gillman | Sam Gilmour | Dom Giossan | Katie Gitelson | Leslie Glazer | Rober

t Grady | Alexander Graefe | Diego Grau | MarieFrance Gravel | Cari Gray | Darren Gray | Tony Gray | Jared Green | Jonathan Green | Marcos Grellet | Elise Grenier | Marc Grenier | Tony Grey

aefer | Philipp Haemmerle | Douglas Hagerman | Chris Hakes | Elaine Hall | Suzanne Hallerman | Amy Halpenny | Tom Hamilton | Doug Hamming | Rosemary Hannam | Meike Hannig | Eve Hanser

eather Hatch | Ruth Hatch | Doris Hausleitner | Christopher Hayes | Kathryn Hayes | Matthew Hayes | Ryan Hayhurst | Janine Hayward | Michael Hayward | Audie Hazenberg | Graydon Hazenberg

Hevia | Astrid Heyerdahl | David Higgins | Larry Hill | Kirsten Hinder | Sveinborg Hlif Gunnarsdottir | Anh Hoang Tran | Kathleen Hobson | Nicholas Hoduk | Sean Hoff | Eileen Holland | Nick Holman

d | Laurel Howard | Leighton Howard | Leah Howe | Norman Howe | Jonathan Hoyte | Jason Hreno | Martin Hrobsky | Erin Huck | Hugh Huddleson | Dorothy Hughes | Kristin Hultsman | Christine

Michelle Isaak | Nancy Ives | Jennifer Ivey **J** Ewa Jablonowska | Craig Jacoby | Nancy Jagger | Ron Jarus | Andrea Jarvis | Paul Jeffery | Susanne Jeffery | Susanne Jeffrey | Jan Jekielek | Car

| Margot Kane | George Kapelos | Jennifer Karch-Verzé | Michael Kasper | Omar Kassis | Georgios Katsikatsos | Celine Kaufman | Panagiota Kavoura | Molly Kellogg | M.T. Kelly | Francis Kelsall

ier Kirby | Jill Kirchmann | Christine Klaassen | Inga-Lill Kleive | Al Kling | Charles Knapp | Olga Kneiflova | Alan Knight | Brenda Knight | Isabelle Knight | Daniel Knott | David Knox | Takuya Kodama

l Labadie | Kate Lacey | Anita Laconagelo | Ethan Lacy | Zoe Lagarde | Augustina Lagos | Remi Lahaussois | Arun Lakra | Judy Lamarsh | Monika Lamm | John Lammers | Kevin Landis | Nathan

e | Danny Legault | Linda Legault | Portia Leggat | Janet Leitch | David Lemanowicz | Christopher Lemieux | Raymond Lemire | Craig Leonard | David Lester | Sharon Levine | David Lewis | John

s | Christopher Litt | Aase Lium | Teresa Liuzzi | Cecilia Ljungman | Greg Lobb | Gina Loes | Chris Lofft | Jennifer Lofft | Alice Loftie | Stefano Lopez | Andreas Logopoulos | Francesco Lombardi

eanna MacDonald | Eve MacDonald | Gillian MacDonald | Jill MacDonald | Jupiter MacDonald | Louise MacDonald | Hugh Macdonnell | Marie MacEwan | Marie Macfarlane | Stan Macfarlane | Tom

Maddox | Michael Madrigale | Trish Magwood | Olivier Maillard | Craig Majernik | Erin Majernik | Alexandre Mallory | Anne Maloney | Kathleen Maloney | Melony Malouf | Tiffany Manchester | Wend

Stephanie Marrone | Anthea Mars | Euan Mars | Katie Marshall | Michael Marshall | Nick Martin | Barbara Martinez | Nuria Martinez | Chris Mason | David Mason | Janice Mason | Michelle Mason

| Thomas McCarthy | Brian McCutcheon | Laura McDaniel | Mary McDerment | Bob McDermott | Tim McDermott | Melissa McDonald | Pamela McDonald | Christine McDougall | David McDouga

enna | Alison McKenzie | Darryl McKenzie | Martha McKimm | Kelly McKinney | Kelly McKinney | Robbin McKinney | Susan McKitrick | Jennifer McLaughlin | Carol McLean | Daniel McLeod | Juli

eredith | Tyler Merringer | Jacques Messe | Diego Metamoros | John Methven | Cindy Meyer | Karena Meyer | Julie Michaux | Elizabeth Miele | Craig Miller | Patricia Miller | Ann Milligan | Nichola

net Moes | Izabella Molenda | Murray Mollard | Maureen Molloy | Sara Monego | Cate Montes | Jennifer Moore |Marianne Moore | Rob Moore | Vicki Moraes | Clare Morawski | Ed Morawski | Dian

| Maeve Muldowney | Julian Mulock | Courtney Mundy | Elaine Munro | Patricia Murer | Daniel Murphy | Fiona Murphy | Norah Murphy | Fulton Murray | Sharon Murray | Suzanne Mustacich | Joh

issa Nelson | Sarah Nelson | Heidi Nesbitt | Marta Nespoli | Ian Newall | Holly Nicholson | Christina Nick |Erika Nigalis | Monica Nissen | Aaron Noble | Mark Nojaim | Heather Nolin | Jennifer Norman

nell | Matthew O'Hara | Breda O'Keefe | Pamela O'Shea | Ted O'Toole | Mickeal Oban | Elizabeth Odell Leroux | Renya Onasick | Kris Ongman | Gabriella Opaz | Patricia Orban | Cheryl Orr | Dugal

ly | Kim Pallozzi | Tom Palmer | Annie-Catherine Parent | Geraldine Parizot | Maria Parolin | Graeme Parry | Silvia Pasqualetti | Riccardo Pasquin | Rachel Patterson | Adrian Paul | Lara Paul | Lucas

hillips | Riccardo Piattelli | Mark Picone | Rob Pierangeli | Martha Pincoffs | Carol Pineau | Mario Plastina | Tamsin Plaxton | Scott Poe | Sophie Poirier | Lindsay Pollard | Timothy Pollock | Eliza Pond

rlo Primiani | Tanya Primiani | Massimo Prioreschi | Dimitri Protogirou | Mark Pruzanski |Veronique Puton **Q** Tracy Quattrocki | Beth Queeney | Dana Quinn **R** Alison Rader | Lisa Rae | Sharon

re Reyes | Kevin Reynolds | Adam Rheborg | Nic Rhind | Annette Riboni | D'Arcy Richardson | Tim Richardson | Claudio Rigatto | Nancy Riley | April Rinne | Kent Riopelle | Gerald Risk | Carl Ritchie

oner | Katherine Robitaille | Dylan Roche | Sarah Rodhouse | Marjolein Roeleveld | Fiona Roeske | Andrew Rogers | Bob Rogers | Clair Rogers | Penny Rogers | Susan Rogers | Lisa Rohe | Mary-C

use | Celine Roussel | Caroline Rousselle | Shannon Rowe | Cathy Roy | Isabelle Roy | James Roy | Andrea Roylance | Jill Rubin | Heather Rumball | Alexiss Rusnak | Claire Russell | Jake Russell

loyd Sacks | Eric Sakalowsky | Barbara Salisbury | Geoff Sandquist | Lesley Sandquist | Lorenzo Santamaria | Isabelle Santoire | Judy Santos | Luis Sarabia | Paola Sartori | Kathleen Saso | Dawn

Sarah Schumann | Angelo Scimia | Charlie Scott | Christian Scott | Christine Scott | Don Scott | Hugh Scott | Yvette Scrivener | Zsanna Sebesteny | Tim Sekold | Kathleen Selkirk | Janet Sellge

ppard | Dale Sherrow | Jennifer Shipley | Tim Shortly | Stephen Siegler | Curt Sigfstead | Todd Sigfstead | Edward Silhol | Geoffrey Simmins | Jody Simmons | Colin Simpson | Laurie Sims | Jonathan

Anna Small | Mark Smye | Aleks Sniatycka | Heidi Sopinka | Anne-Marie Sorrenti | Esta Spalding | Amy Sparrow | Edward Spat | Nicola Speakman | Kimberly Spilker | Susan Spinale | Eric Sponselle

art | Kathy Stewart | Kellan Stewart | Rachel Stewart | Richard Stewart | Ruth Stewart | Steven Stichter | Gino Stinziani | Peter Stock | Caroline Stockdale | Erin Stokes | Steve Stollerman | Barbara

es | Matthew Swarney | Bob Sweet | Eric Sylvers **T** Chris Tabbitt | Ted Talley | Laura Tamblyn | Roxanne Tanase | Rock Tang | Mallory Tarses | Martin Taticek | Michelle Tawharu | Andrew Taylo

n Threatt | Ron Tice | Marco Timpano | Michael Torrey | Walter Tovell | Nancy Towns | Judy Tredgett | Dane Tredway | Duff Trimble | Christopher Truffa | Jerome Truran | Muriel Truter | Christine

t | Jackie Van Hees | Jacquie Van Ierssel | Sarah van Nostrand | Abby van Oers | Debbie Vanvaerenbergh | George Vassos | Sebastian Vautelin | Neva Vehovec | Megan Verchere | Maria Verdicchio

uth | Nicola von Shroeter | Gerlinde Voppichler | Juan Vuotto **W** Alyson Walker | Angela Walker | Jim Walker | Kim Walker | Sandy Walker | Gwyn Wansbrough | Robin Wark | Genevieve Warwic

gust | Eugenie Weiss | Richard Weiss | George Wells | Heather Wells | Jennifer Welsh | Kristin Wesoloski | Anne West | Elizabeth Wetzel | Sarah Wheeler | Peter Whish | Richard White | Robert White

DO YOU KNOW
THE WAY TO
MONTRACHET
(1968)

"We're like swans – we may look elegant, but we're paddling like hell underwater."

UNKNOWN

4

1994
-
2000 A Higher Gear

"You're an itinerant dilettante"

With more than five million daily riders, the odds of bumping into someone you know in the New York City subway are slim. So it was no small surprise for Michael Liss, a B&R guide temporarily settled in New York and working on his master's degree in interactive telecommunications, to see George Butterfield riding a subway escalator in the opposite direction on a brisk January day in 1993. "Talk about coincidences," says Michael. "I don't even *take* the subway. I'm a taxi person."

Michael had guided biking trips for B&R in Italy for two seasons. The company was a perfect fit for his background and interests. All through his childhood and early teens, he and his family had lived and travelled around the world, following his father's career as an executive at Procter & Gamble. Along the way Michael developed a passion for art and culture, an eye for design, and a taste for nice hotels. "I had spent ten years playing around in life," Michael recalls, "and when I got the job guiding for B&R, my dad said, 'Finally, a job where you have the perfect qualifications. You're an itinerant dilettante.'"

Crossing paths with George in the subway that day reminded Michael how much he missed travelling – and it sparked an idea. Maybe he could convince B&R to send him on a research trip. Drawing on his personal travels, Michael had casually pitched trip ideas to B&R before, but this time he made a special effort to prepare a detailed,

thoughtful, and convincing proposal for a one-week biking trip through Spain's Andalucia region. "Basically, I just wanted a free trip," he admits.

When Michael's suggested itinerary reached the B&R office, George's response was immediate and enthusiastic. He waved the proposal around, implored everyone to read it, and asked the pointed question: "Why isn't anyone else writing stuff like this?" Though Michael had never actually been to Andalucia, he'd written the itinerary as though the trip already existed, evocatively describing each day at length – what the experience of biking through the countryside would look like, smell like, feel like. Not everyone was thrilled about the proposal's instant acclaim, but George knew instinctively it was gold. As things turned out, he sent a European-based guide off to research the Andalucian trip, and before long Michael was on his way to map out a new itinerary in Belize.

Planning a great trip is one thing, but getting people excited enough to sign up for it is another. On this tricky part of the business, Michael had fresh and persuasive views. "He got talking to me about the marketing and started to make a lot of sense," says George. As much as anything, it was Michael's clear and simple way of seeing things that resonated with George. After two years of increasing frustration with the way B&R's marketing was being handled, George had found a fresh talent – someone he trusted to communicate the B&R message.

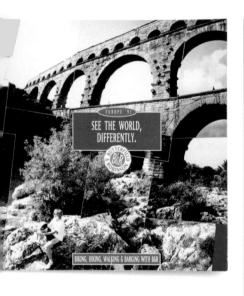

Feeling out of touch with George's renewed vision for B&R and hamstrung in his role as president, Danny Legault resigned in the summer of 1993 and left to pursue a technology venture. A few months later, after a tense and terse dinner in Beaune (at which George informed Tom Hamilton that Michael would be assuming responsibility for the production of the 1994 brochure), Tom and B&R parted ways. The business was shifting gears, and the cast of characters was changing.

From the beginning, B&R had always put a lot of effort into creating beautiful brochures. Throughout the sixties and seventies the look was minimalist yet strong – artful black and white photos, straightforward graphics, and fuss-free fonts. In the eighties Tom loosened the design language and filled the brochures with plenty of bright, colourful photography and original, often whimsical cover art.

By the time George asked Michael to help with B&R's marketing in the fall of 1993, the message, visual and verbal, had become something of a hodgepodge. "It was so complex what the company was offering," remembers Michael. Adult biking, hiking, walking, cross-country skiing, rafting, and barging trips in Europe, North America, and a handful of exotic countries elsewhere; a few student trips; an Arctic adventure; and a hosted villa rental program called Homes Away.

ABOVE
Newspaper clippings from the eighties

BELOW
Be careful when tightrope walking above a bicycle

"I looked for a unifying thread that defined the company," he says, "and I realized that we always biked or walked on these trips, if only for a day." Paring everything back to the basics, Michael grounded the idea of Butterfield & Robinson with two succinct lines that explained not just *what* the company did but *how* and *why*.

Biking & Walking Since 1966

Slow Down to See the World

There was no magic to the words (*slow* had been part of the B&R vernacular for a decade or more), but the clarity and simplicity of the message was exactly what George was looking for.

Seeking to develop a fresh voice and visual identity for B&R, Michael scrapped the brochure that was already underway and set out to find a new design studio. He settled on a small Toronto company called Viva Dolan, a recently formed partnership between graphic designer / illustrator Frank Viva and writer Doug Dolan. "Take an outsider's view," Michael told them. And they did. "I remember we brought in a big, square oversized format that was so anti-catalogue," recalls Frank. "On one page was a tiny photograph of a tree in the centre of this field of black, and Michael was blown away by it. "Oh my God, I *love* it!" he said. And that was that.

Butterfield & Robinson Travel

Butterfield & Robinson

the Loire

...eld ...inson
...ND WALKING SINCE 1966

...erfield &Robinson
...KING AND WALKING SINCE 1966

"Oh my God, I love it!"

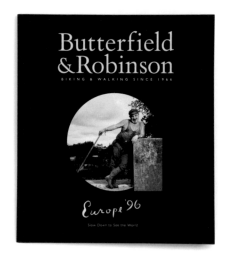

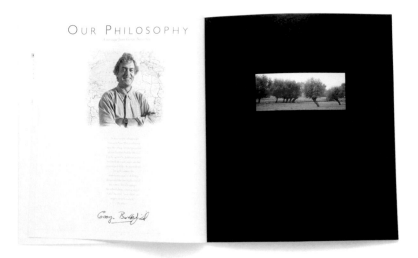

Together, Michael, Frank, and Doug shaped a brand expression that elevated B&R through smart, snappy copy, innovative design, and stunning photography. Up to that point the company brochures had primarily used stock photos and guide snapshots. They were often fun but seldom gorgeous. By hiring professional photographers and sending them each year on carefully planned two-week shoots in Europe, B&R was able get spectacular images of guides, hotels, bikers, walkers, events, and serendipitous moments – the elements that made the B&R experience special and precisely what they wanted to market. "We'd sit up all night working on those trip pages," says Michael. "We'd choose the photos together and come up with captions that really cracked us up. 'Did we really say that?' But once you put something in writing, it's not so outrageous anymore. Everyone takes it for granted."

Visual punch was important, but the subtler goal was to suggest an attitude, an approach – not just to travel but to life. "We built an aesthetic around B&R and applied a sensibility that was reflective of George and Martha," says Frank. That was the key – to convey a spirit of adventure and generosity that was somehow inclusive and yet exclusive at the same time. By making George the poster boy –

"this incredible bon vivant travel guru," as Michael puts it – B&R was able to communicate the personality of the company in a genuine and appealing way. It was an easy message to sell.

To be fair, by the mid-nineties it was becoming easier to peddle a biking or a walking trip. What had been a revolutionary idea when B&R introduced the first adult bike trip in 1980 was gradually moving into the mainstream. The market had expanded exponentially. Active travel was now the zeitgeist, and although B&R was at the forefront, a growing pack of competitors was eagerly filling the slipstream – Backroads, VBT (Vermont Bicycle Touring), Travent, Country Walkers, and more. "We didn't notice it at the time," says George. "We were doing so well we weren't paying much attention to the others. I thought we should simply do our own thing, focusing on what we do and how we could do it better."

Notwithstanding a nonchalant attitude to its competition, B&R felt a deep responsibility to its travellers – and they too were evolving. "At first they were people who were in for adventure, who loved to bike and knew what they were getting in for," reflects Martha. "But increasingly they developed expectations of American comforts in

Au Revoir, Les Glycines

For at least 10,000 years, stylish and comfortable lodgings have been important. In 1868 a geologist named Louis Lartet found five skeletons in a cave in southwestern France. Remarkably, the Cro-Magnon specimens he discovered were the remains of the earliest known race of modern humans. Equally amazing, the prehistoric dwelling was adorned with their artwork – fabulous polychromatic cave paintings of mammoths, horses, and bison.

Just a short walk away, in the small town of Les-Eyzies-de-Tayac-Sireuil (let's just call it Les Eyzies), is Hôtel Les Glycines. For years a fixture on B&R biking and walking trip in the Dordogne region, Les Glycines was the sort of hotel George and Martha loved. "The owner was so special, the

Europe and everywhere they went. Those demands kept pushing the bar higher." B&R had always taken pride in running the best possible trips. Now, with the travel market and clientele maturing, "best" was becoming synonymous with high-end.

When Michael first suggested that B&R should define itself as a *luxury* active travel company, George had an "uneasy feeling" and resisted the gilded terminology. Always one to favour a rich experience over an expensive one, he didn't want B&R travellers to stay only in fancy hotels. He wanted to share the charm and personality of smaller inns – even if they were a little quirky at times. But Michael was persuasive in his argument, insisting that if their travellers wanted high-end hotels and experiences, B&R would be wise to deliver luxury. After several impromptu lunch meetings at the Senator Restaurant, a classic diner around the corner from the office, George agreed that B&R should reach for the top.

In addition to his talent for marketing, Michael had an innate understanding of B&R's predominantly American traveller base. More than 85 percent of its travellers now came from the United States. Even though he was soon working full time in Toronto as B&R's marketing director, Michael, an American himself, continued to live in New York City, commuting to Toronto every Monday and

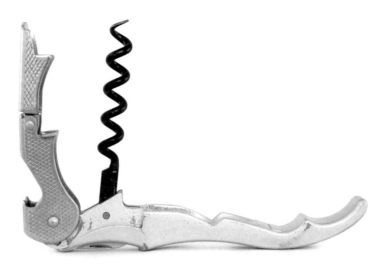

LEFT
*Jean-Louis
Bottigliero
welcomes B&R to
Château de Gilly
in Burgundy*

ABOVE
*The only tool you
ever really need*

restaurant was excellent, the garden was gorgeous, the location was ideal – it was a lovely little place," says George. Charming, yes, but not perfect. "It was so uneven," remembers Peter Smale, head of European trip planning at the time. "There were some great rooms and some tiny former maid rooms. And most of the mattresses were kind of lumpy. It could work beautifully, or it could be a total headache for the guides."

"Our job was to stay in the lead and keep upping the ante," Michael Liss asserts. As much as George wanted the itineraries to include a variety of hotels, B&R travellers had come to expect the best – the very best. While visiting a group staying at Les Glycines in the fall of 1995, George heard the demand for luxury first hand. "This guy called me over during cocktails and hauled me up to see his room," he recalls. "'You expect me to stay in this kind of room?' the man asked, pointing to the bed. 'This is just impossible! I can't live in a room like this!'"

flying home to Manhattan for the weekend. Constant exposure to the world beyond B&R's office on Bond Street kept the company in tune and added a dash of boldness. Amy Fisher, who began in the mailroom but quickly moved up to the marketing department, puts it this way: "We were conservative Canadians who didn't like to push the envelope, and Michael would say, 'No, there *is* an appetite for this idea – there *is* a market.'"

George and Michael set the tempo with a crisp vision and a captivating message, but it was an orchestra of many that made the music. Directly supporting the marketing push was a small team of people who ensured that everything going out the door, whether a t-shirt, a corkscrew, or a set of on-trip materials, consistently reflected the B&R brand in tone and design. Broadcasting the word was Cari Gray, B&R's self-styled one-woman PR machine, whose ability to track down almost any writer or magazine editor was matched by a willingness to hop on a plane and go to see them. Reflecting on Michael's leadership style, she recalls, "He was demanding to work with, but he sure had the vision." And every day the vision spread further. Though Canada and the United States remained B&R's largest markets, the enthusiasm of Rio de Janeiro-based traveller and entrepreneur Marcia Lucas was rapidly putting B&R on the map in Brazil.

When the phones rang, which they did a lot, a group of young and energetic travel advisers (invariably led by someone marginally less young and doubly energetic) was there to field questions about the difference between hills in Tuscany and in Provence. And when travellers were ready to book, Picard, the initially troublesome reservation system Danny had implemented, was all set to capture the information. Slowly, B&R was becoming more organized, more efficient.

Shocked and sweating from this awkward conversation, George realized the time had come for B&R to say goodbye to Les Glycines. "He was totally torn up by that," says Peter Smale. "The alternatives were heartless, soulless places that made George's skin crawl. His values are completely sincere and true. For him it's all about authenticity and originality and looking at the world in a new way. And here he was butting up against another fact of life – if you want to run a serious travel business, you need to keep the travellers seriously happy."

It was a sad ending to a treasured relationship, but a few weeks later the owners of Les Glycines sent George and Martha a letter that ended with these words: "Surtout sans amertume" – Above all without bitterness.

Everyone was now figuring out how to operate in the new environment where bridled enthusiasm was clearly more powerful than running around in circles. To counterbalance George's potentially disruptive zest for new ideas, managers followed an unspoken policy: "If George didn't say it three times, we didn't raise a finger," says Chris Tabbitt, the sales manager at the time. While there was a concerted effort to help the business mature, there was an equal respect for keeping it young. "I was trying to put things in a structure and format that was more regular, without killing the goose," recalls Peter Smale, who, over the nineties, worked his way from guide to trip planner to managing director. "We were still giving people the go-ahead to run great trips and do crazy things, but everything was much more accountable and anticipated. It was a steady curve."

The financial predictability was also welcomed. Better budgeting, favourable foreign exchange rates, and an effort by guides to be somewhat respectful of the new trip spending guideline (TSG) added up to a reliable profit, year after year. At last, George and Martha's house could be taken off the balance sheet. And although the bottom line was never a distraction for them, it was nice not to have to think about it so much. "Businesses that are doing well are fun," reflects George, "whereas those that are struggling financially are not as much fun."

LEFT
Students letting loose at the end of an epic biking journey

ABOVE
The sun setting over the Sahara as travellers make their way to a tented camp

In the summer of 1994 B&R made the decision to run its final student trip. Participant numbers had been slipping slowly, and a change in Ontario's education policy meant that B&R's academic adventures were no longer eligible for a course credit. It was a heartbreaker, but just a few months later a wildcard trip idea more than made up for the loss.

Following a hunch that B&R's loyal band of travellers was ready to embrace a wider offering of exotic biking and walking trips, and hoping to round out the business with some winter trips, Michael hopped on a plane to Morocco to check it out. It took just five days and a chance meeting with Frederick "Frecky" Vreeland, the United States ambassador to Morocco at the time and son of the fabled *Vogue* editor-in-chief Diana Vreeland, to convince him that he'd found trip-planning gold in the Sahara. With the help of Frank and Doug at Viva Dolan, Michael produced a tantalizing brochure.

Muriel Truter, George's personal assistant who had been moonlighting in the marketing department, remembers walking into George's office with Michael to present the mini masterpiece. "He gave us that sideways nod, effectively saying, 'It'll never sell.'" Grabbing paper and pencil from George's desk, Michael began to sketch Bedouin tents, sand dunes, Land Rovers, and camels. "He didn't want dusty old

In just two years Morocco became B&R's most popular trip anywhere in the world and remained so until 2001

Moroccan camels," laughs Muriel. "He wanted camels decked out with regalia." As things happened, a lot of people were keen to ride bikes *and* camels. In just two years Morocco became B&R's most popular trip anywhere in the world and remained so until 2001. "It was a real watershed," says Cari. "We were the first to take people biking there and had a monopoly for the longest time."

In short order, under a newly minted banner Expeditions, other colourful trips were added in Asia, Africa, and Latin America. Nathalie Butterfield, George and Martha's daughter, who had guided a few seasons in Europe and had just finished her law degree, agreed to spread the word to B&R's most frequent travellers. Her characteristically unconventional marketing mission was to spend a week apiece in Hong Kong, Nepal, and India and send something fun from each place to all 250 names on the list. "It was totally left up to me to be creative," says Nathalie, "but it had to be really personal." In Hong Kong she prepared packages containing local coins, red plastic dragons, and trinkets from the market. Wrapped in Chinese newspaper and addressed with hand-written labels, the packages certainly made an impact when they arrived stateside. "A bunch of people called the B&R office to make sure they didn't have a bomb in their mailbox," she remembers with a smile.

The Expedition trips broadened B&R's reach, underscored its commitment to innovation, and allowed the company to stay a step ahead of the competition. But Europe remained B&R's bread and cheese, still accounting for more than 80 percent of all trips. Just as in the Toronto office, the operational machine in Beaune (eventually with depots in Ireland and in Arezzo, Italy) rose to the challenge of researching, planning, and delivering more trips every year.

In the winter months, when there were no European trips, a small crew of full-time coordinators and trip planners led by the optimistic and open-minded Vicky Bake negotiated leases for dozens of white vans, prepared guide manuals, and called around or visited the

··················
PREVIOUS
*Intensely urban
Fez and blissfully
spare Argentina*

BELOW
*En route to the
Consulate*

RIGHT
*Unlocked and
loaded, ready to
hit the road*

BOTTOM RIGHT
*B&R's 1994 Official
Bicycle Registry*

A Night in NYC

Sandwiched between a pair of bland yellow-brick apartment blocks on Fifth Avenue, directly across the street from New York's Central Park, sits the stout yet stately home of the Consulate General of France. Built in the early years of last century for an American banker, the Italian Renaissance-style townhouse is the sort of place people walk by and wonder, "What goes on in there?"

In search of an address that would hold mystery and prestige, Michael Liss chose it as the venue for a B&R event in January 1995. From the beginning, B&R combined traditional print advertising with spreading the word in person in schools and living rooms. By the mid-nineties the marketing strategy had evolved to include a series of lively presentations in key cities across the United States

hundreds of hotels and suppliers B&R relied on to make each itinerary special – goat cheese makers in the Loire, wood marquetry workshops in Alsace, fiddlers on the Aran Islands, bullfighters in Seville, and ceramics studios in Tuscany. Every relationship was real and every one of them mattered.

By late March, seasonal staff would start to trickle in. Thousands of B&R travellers, from the Upper East Side to West Hollywood, were busy packing Gore-Tex jackets and ExOfficio convertible pants (shants) into ballistic-grade black nylon Tumi bags. They would be arriving soon – with mounting expectations of top-tier gear and impeccable route notes. There was work to be done. Upping the equipment ante for the 1994 season, B&R took delivery of a fleet of custom-made Trek bicycles – each one of them painted deep purple, decked with branded handlebar bags, and stencilled with an individual name relating to some place or thing from the B&R world. The Gordes Galloper, Foie Gras Flyer, Rhine River Ripper. Why miss a chance to flash some creativity?

Keeping the chains greased and the gears shifting smoothly was a relentless chore, but the gang of bike mechanics (*les mecs*), as many as fifteen in peak season, somehow made it look easy – and fun. Jimmy McGavin, head of the equipment atelier, led the charge to Pickwick's

and Canada. Typically hosted by George, Martha, Michael, and a handful of B&R guides and staff, the evenings invariably attracted enthusiastic crowds of current and potential travellers.

"I don't remember what the capacity of the consulate was," says Michael, "but we weren't counting our RSVPs very well. All we wanted was an approximate head count so we could order sufficient hors d'oeuvres and drinks." The French consulate, however, asked precisely how many people were coming. The elegant *Salon Rose* that B&R had hired for the evening, staff said, could accommodate 150 people. At that point, given the large turnout at earlier presentations, George suspected that space at the consulate might get a little tight.

Doors opened at 6:00 pm. "By about 6:15 pm the place was full, and people were lined up down Fifth Avenue and around the corner," he remembers.

"There had to be five or six hundred people." Kelly McKinney, one of the B&R hosts that evening, describes the scene inside: "People were pouring into the room, fighting for chairs and lining the back walls. We'd shut the doors, do a presentation, and try to herd them out of the building before the next wave arrived."

George, meanwhile, took to the sidewalk to apologize to the crowd. "I walked out there and said, 'This is not a rock concert – it's Butterfield & Robinson. I'm sorry, but there's no more room and you're not going to get in.' At which point people went crazy. They began pushing their way through the door, and the French consulate was in a complete twist. It was an absolute madhouse."

When the dust settled the following day, B&R realized the disastrous event had inadvertently been perfectly planned. "New Yorkers love a thing they can't get into," says Michael. "Then they *really* want to be a part of it."

To make amends with the consulate, B&R delivered a pair of brand new bikes.

Pub in Beaune most nights and rarely left before laughing himself hoarse (and receiving a nudge from the bartender to go home so they could lock the door).

Things kicked into high gear in early May with the annual guide gathering. The primary purpose was to bring everyone together (old guides, new guides, bike mechanics, the European operations team, and a handful of people from the Toronto office) to ensure that the unique culture of the company was well communicated and kept alive.

There were always group bike rides and walks, with many a wrong turn as everyone assumed that somebody else was following the route notes. There were also casual chats about essential topics: how best to engineer "WOW scenarios" (unplanned moments of magic), pull together the ultimate picnic, or open Champagne bottles with a sabre. George or Martha, usually both, attended these gatherings to help set the tone, pass along the company's history, and calibrate the creativity – ensuring that the fun was somewhat wild, but not totally out of control.

Kelly McKinney, who led trips and later worked as a manager in Toronto for many years, remembers a spirited guide gathering at the Royal Saltworks of Arc-et-Senans, an eighteenth-century architectural masterpiece in the French countryside. "After dinner, we all decided to take our clothes off and form a massive human sundial by lying down on the grass of this huge semi-circular courtyard. Back in the office the following Monday, George called me aside: 'Hey, great

> **"The guides represented what B&R wanted people in the world to be–unfailingly optimistic, friendly, open-minded, and always with a resourceful, can-do attitude"**

··················
ABOVE LEFT
Equipe Butterfield moments after winning the 24 heures de Beaune bike race

ABOVE
George, the sabre-sleuth tiger

ABOVE RIGHT
Kelly McKinney kicking off the craziness at the Arc-et-Senans guide gathering

party, fantastic sun dial," he said, "but when you returned to the party naked, that sort of crossed the line.'"

As B&R got itself more organized in the nineties, guide training also became a more elaborate and considered affair. Due time was allotted to bike tuning, trip accounting workshops, and van training (whipping through small streets in a large van with twenty-four bikes on the roof isn't easy). Rookie guides were encouraged to read the detailed guide manual carefully, "then throw it away." Ultimately, what B&R was trying to communicate was a hard thing to teach – how to balance fun with responsibility, local expertise with a sense of place, confidence with graciousness. "In some sense," comments

ABOVE
Phillippe Brown preparing a colourful t-shirt presentation

ABOVE RIGHT
Nicky Speakman, the guide hiring guru

BOTTOM RIGHT
Five-star service, six-star smile

Roger Martin, former dean of the Rotman School of Management and long-time member of B&R's Advisory Board, "the guides represented what B&R wanted people in the world to be like – unfailingly optimistic, friendly, open-minded, and always with a resourceful, can-do attitude. They were dedicated to a good time being had by all."

Of the guides, Martha says, "Sidney, George, and I used to look at each other and say, 'And we thought we couldn't clone ourselves! These people are easily as good as we ever were.'" B&R exerted a strong gravitational pull on like-minded souls and attracted vast numbers of eager applicants desperate to guide for the company. If anyone can take credit for guarding the spark and passing it on, it is Nicola Speakman, B&R's guide coordinator from 1987 to 2005. Nicky, as everyone knew her, had an uncanny sense for knowing who would be a good fit and who would not. "She interviewed so many people," says Amy Fisher, "yet made very, very few mistakes." Because many guiding gigs evolved into other roles, it's fair to say that Nicky hired at least a third of all the people who have worked at B&R over the past fifty years.

Ask anyone who made it through the gates, and they'll tell a similar story. "I wanted it so badly," admits Cari, "my face was sweating all through the interview." Sitting calmly behind her desk, long

salt-and-pepper hair framing a Mona Lisa facial expression, Nicky was impossible to read. She made the person in the chair opposite feel totally at ease, yet bewildered too. "Why isn't she asking me to speak Italian?" the nervous candidates wondered. "What does my choice of undergraduate studies have to do with guiding bike trips?"

Nicky knew that being a great guide had little to do with mechanical skills, administrative aptitude, or hiking prowess. She was looking for people who would be fun and interesting to travel with, individuals with character, knowledge, relentless curiosity, and an uncommon level of grace. It didn't matter if you were an architect, artist, philosopher, doctor, lawyer, mathematician, or concert pianist. You just had to be brilliant with people – or as George says, "the ultimate host, the ultimate leader." As much as B&R valued and appreciated their guides, it was the travellers who had the final say. Invariably the feedback boiled down to five glowing words: "The guides made the trip."

Not surprisingly, the guides were more than happy to make the trip. Even with the exhaustingly long hours and modest pay, guiding for B&R was an exceptionally rewarding experience – an opportunity to eat, drink, and sleep way beyond one's means, a chance to hang out with fascinating and accomplished travellers, and an excuse to explore the world up close and at length. "It was like a never ending cocktail

"Now *that* was worth the price of admission"

party," says Dave Swales, who started as a bike mechanic in 1989 and subsequently guided more than one hundred student and adult trips for B&R. Though sometimes very challenging, leading trips was almost always fun for the simple reason that the guides had the freedom and the resources to make every day as magical as possible.

Dave remembers a powerful moment on the second day of the inaugural bike trip in Vietnam in 1996, a journey he helped to create. Instead of driving from Hanoi to Halong Bay, he arranged for the group to cover the 160 kilometre (100 mile) distance in enormous Mi-17 Russian helicopters. "We were flying over the treetops, with the windows open," he remembers, "so low you could see the faces of people in the villages. It was like reliving a news clip from the Vietnam War. When the helicopters landed, no one said a word – they were all so overwhelmed." Eventually, a traveller walked up to him and exclaimed, "Now *that* was worth the price of admission."

As might be expected, many guides developed close relationships with one another. "It was a remarkable collection of people with a common *joie de vivre*," says Georgia Yuill, "people who enjoyed being out of their comfort zone." After leading trips in Italy for three seasons, Georgia married a fellow guide, Graeme Parry, and moved with him to Milan, where they currently live with their children and she continues to plan trips for B&R. By conservative math, no fewer than thirty couples have emerged from the guide pool, and they, in turn, have added twice that many children to B&R's extended family.

LEFT
*Boarding the
big bird for
Halong Bay*

BELOW
*Small car,
big love*

Over the course of the nineties the relationship between B&R and its guides also evolved and grew more serious. The abundance of new trips and destinations every year translated to a steady stream of opportunity and a matching need for guides who were available to work longer stretches and make deeper commitments to the company. Whereas most guides in the eighties had other full-time jobs at home and slipped away for a few weeks as a kind of subsidized European vacation, many guides in the nineties began leading trips in different countries around the world and throughout the year. Guiding became a possible career path, and for some the role expanded to include trip planning and research.

In 1997 a young guide named Norman Howe was hired to work full time in the Toronto office and asked to find a way to manage the complexity of operating hundreds of trips in myriad destinations. His solution led to the regional director program – an organizational structure that matched experienced guides with a portfolio of trips.

Norm connected with B&R in the first place through his love of travel and his ability on the squash court. While articling at Torys in Toronto he got an unexpected call from one of the corner-office partners, Sidney Robinson, asking if he would be his squash partner for the day.

Georgia and Graeme
June 21, 2000

Where were you on December 31, 1999?

Sidney explained that his regular partner was away on business, and he'd heard that Norm was good on the court. "I played horribly and we lost," says Norm. "I was in the dog house and could see my law career arc coming to an end." But a couple of weeks later, when Sidney's partner was away again, Norm got another call. This time, they won. "Sidney liked me after that," Norm chuckles. A couple of years later, when Norm decided that practising law wasn't his thing after all, Sidney suggested he have lunch with George. Norm "had no idea who George was at that point," but he ended up guiding his first trip for B&R in 1995. Sidney's instinct for picking a partner proved to be right on.

Well before Michael Liss's chance meeting with George on the New York subway, he had harboured a dream of creating an exclusive wilderness retreat. "He wanted to put his mark on the world independently of anyone else," says Frank Viva. After six years of running B&R in perfect sync with George, brilliantly crafting the marketing message and astutely steering the trip planning machine, Michael's enthusiasm was drifting to the Southwest.

At the same time, business at B&R was booming, each year breaking new sales records. "When you grow quickly," says Paul Christopher, B&R's chief financial officer for over twenty years, "and you have more people doing more and more stuff, there's a much greater need for leadership." From the start, Michael's prodigious talent for tuning a vision was never matched by a commensurate knack for management. And increasingly, that's what George (and others) felt B&R needed most. "People were telling George he'd run the course of his capability

"He has a sensibility that is rare. You're not taught these things in corporate America"

to grow the business as a visionary and entrepreneur," says Peter Smale. "They told him to bring in professionals to run the company."

And that's exactly what he did. In the fall of 1999, just as Michael stepped away to pursue his dream, George hired Gil Roberts as B&R's new chief operating officer and managing director. A long-time B&R traveller with an appreciation for the company's soft and fuzzy culture, Gil was also a bona fide business guy with impressive experience at Sara Lee and the Russell Corporation.

Norm remembers how things unfolded: "George was going to be the visionary, and Gil the execution guy. But in reality, when someone gets a leadership role in the business, George and Martha expect that person to fill the creative side too." For Gil, working for a privately owned company was an eye-opening experience. "You learn that whatever is going through the entrepreneur's head is top of mind," he says. After little more than a year, the experiment came to an amicable end. Gil resigned, and George put one hand back on the helm. "I am a completely different person today than I was before I went to work for George," comments Gil. "He has a sensibility that is rare. You're not taught these things in corporate America."

B&R has never behaved like a large, traditional company. But as it crested the millennium, it was bigger, brighter, and stronger than ever. By numbers, the picture could hardly have been rosier. Bookings hit another record high, as did profits. In B&R's typically generous fashion, the bounty was shared with all the employees through a profit-share plan that amounted to bonus cheques for as much as 40 percent of base salary. Muriel Truter remembers chatting with Massimo Prioreschi, the sales and IT manager during the period, on their way back from lunch one day. "He had just taken his profit-share cheque to the bank," she explained, "and he asked the teller to give it to him all in cash because he had never seen that much money in his life before." In the span of seven years, B&R's Toronto office had grown from seventeen to more than fifty full-time staff.

Though a number of investors expressed interest in buying the company, George, Martha, and Sidney had no interest in selling – not even for the stratospheric multiples offered. They were not in it for the money. The real return on their decades-long investment of time and energy was consistently delivering extraordinary trips for all the travellers and guides.

Ever mindful of the need to keep innovating to stay ahead of the herd, B&R launched two new programs in 2000. One, Rivers & Oceans, offered travellers the opportunity to camp in style and relative luxury amid pristine wilderness on rafting journeys that followed some of the great Canadian West Coast rivers. The other, By Sea, took to the open waters and developed a series of ship-based luxury biking and walking trips through the Mediterranean and along Scotland's Hebridean coast. The underlying idea behind both trips was the same – to travel in a creative way that would allow an unusually rewarding degree of magic to happen. Sakis Mitsoulis, who has guided B&R By Sea trips for more than a dozen years, cites the unpredictability of the itineraries as the secret to their success. "There's this incredible sense of adventure because you never know where the wind will take you," he says. "You experience travel through the eyes of mythological figures. Everything is liquid."

Reflecting on that remarkably golden era, Peter says: "We caught the right wave at the right time. And we took advantage of it." As B&R sailed into 2001, it was nothing but blue sky ahead.

Teed Up

For years, B&R has been coming up with colourful t-shirt designs. And for almost as long, guides have been coming up with creative ways to hand them out to travellers. These are a few classic tee tales.

SPECIAL TEES

It's All in the Delivery

THE BOGGLER | A

Wearing all twenty t-shirts for the group, a guide buries herself in a peat bog on Ireland's west coast, popping out of the ground just as the travellers walk by on their way to lunch. "I think I just soiled my shirt."

THE SMASH HIT | B

A traditional Rajasthani dancer balancing half a dozen clay pots on her head trips mid-performance. As she falls to the floor, the pots go flying and smash to pieces revealing the t-shirts hidden inside. "I hope those weren't her best pots."

A

D

THE HIDDEN BLESSING

While visiting a monastery on the Peloppenese in Greece, travellers encounter a monk washing his clothes in the river, only to discover the monk is their guide and his clothes are their t-shirts. "That was the coolest wet t-shirt ever, no contest."

C

THE BARREL OF FUN

Hermetically sealed in a barrel and thrown into the sea off the coast of Capri, a batch of t-shirts wait for the travellers to help the captain pull up a 'tangled' anchor. "Well, that was a little overboard."

D

THE SMOKE SHOW

A guide's magician boyfriend joins the group for lunch and puts on an impromptu performance, somehow making the t-shirts appear from a ball of fire. "Good thing they used t-shirts, not rabbits."

E

C

B

E

THE VIENNA WALTZER
DEM WIENNER WALDER
(1868)

---

*"You can't wait for
inspiration, you have to
go after it with a club."*

JACK LONDON

5

2001 - 2011

Turbulence

Yonge-Dundas Square in downtown Toronto sits at the intersection of two of the city's main thoroughfares – Yonge and Dundas streets. Always busy and hyper-illuminated with neon, it is Canada's answer to New York's Times Square. Less than a minute's walk east is Bond Street, a calming three-block stretch that's as discreet as the square is ebullient.

And yet, for all its low-key leafiness, Bond Street has plenty to show and tell. At one end of the street is the campus of Ryerson University (Canada's tenth largest university), an austere-looking Lutheran Church with a super-sized organ, and a Greek Orthodox Church with masterfully painted iconography on the interior. At the other end is St. Michael's Hospital and the enormous neo-Gothic Metropolitan United Church. In the middle of the street, right next to another impressive church (St. Michael's Cathedral), is a boys' choir school. Across the street is an elegant Georgian townhouse that was the final home of Toronto's first mayor and 1837 revolutionary leader, William Lyon Mackenzie. A few doors down, at 70 Bond Street, is the Canadian home of Butterfield & Robinson.

Although the five-storey brick and stone heritage building has a small elevator, anyone going up to the B&R office on the third floor will take the stairs – carefully pacing themselves on the creaking wooden steps so they won't appear out of breath when they reach

9/11

ABOVE
*The Butterfield
& Robinson
office at 70
Bond Street*

their destination. A large penny-farthing bicycle and stack of vintage leather luggage in the reception area provide the first clues that this workplace isn't exactly business as usual. There are eight glass-walled offices, including George's den-like corner suite, but otherwise the space is open and bright, informal and cozy. Lead-paned windows filter light into an informal meeting room at the front of the building. It was here that dozens of staff crowded around a diminutive 13-inch television, stuffed into an antique pine armoire, and watched the world change on the morning of September 11, 2001.

The day before, in the same room, senior managers had gathered around the table to meet with a consultant who had been engaged to assess the status quo and provide insight. "She asked if we could foresee any disruptions affecting the business," recalls Kelly McKinney. "We said, 'No, we have a great track record and we've been growing like crazy – nothing can stop us.' And then the next day – Boom!"

Like many people watching the catastrophe unfold in New York, no one at B&R was sure what to make of the horror they were seeing on the small screen. "Then the phone rang," says George, "and the first person called to cancel a trip. I was a bit stunned that they would cancel. I remember trying to convince them to travel. I didn't quite understand what was going on." An hour later another traveller

A Gentleman and an Officer

In 1967, one year after Butterfield & Robinson was born, Queen Elizabeth II established the Order of Canada to "recognize outstanding achievement, dedication to the community and service to the nation." It's Canada's highest civilian honour for lifetime achievement and, as such, a pretty big deal.

Quite apart from being insatiably curious, George is ridiculously generous – with his time, his energy, and yes, his money. Beyond his obvious contributions to the world of travel, he and Martha have long (and often very quietly) supported a wide range of causes and organizations – the World Wildlife Fund, Ecojustice, World Literacy of Canada, PEN Canada (which defends freedom of expression as a basic human right), Coach House Press, and a slew of museums, galleries, and cultural centres.

It was George's involvement with the Ontario College of Art and Design (now OCAD University) which put an extra shine on his philanthropic profile and led to his being named an Officer of the Order of Canada in 2006. As chairperson of OCAD's capital campaign, he helped to raise over $40 million for the institution, much of which was used for the construction of the Sharp Centre for Design – a modernist shoebox with a black and white checkerboard facade. Most noticeable about this avant-garde structure are the dozen multicoloured steel legs that prop the building four-storeys above the ground – like a giant tabletop on chopsticks.

Underneath the dramatic architecture is a modest public space called Butterfield Park – a perfect spot to share ideas and ponder creativity, all to make the world a nicer place.

called to cancel – then another and another. B&R staff weren't sure what to say, but they had to say something. At 4:00 pm George and the managers decided that B&R would run all the upcoming trips, whether they had two travellers or twenty-four. There would be no refunds, but they would allow travellers to cancel and roll a 50 percent credit over to the following year.

By mid-morning of the following day, it was obvious that the situation was much more severe and considerably more complex than anyone had thought. Calls from concerned travellers flooded the office. Autumn had always been the peak travel period for B&R, but 2001 was acutely busy: September 12 marked the single busiest day of the year, with more trips and travellers on the road than ever before. Further intensifying the situation was the fact that New York was the biggest city of origin for B&R travellers, and this tragedy was affecting them profoundly and personally. "The rawness of the emotion coming at us was overwhelming," recalls Norm Howe.

B&R realized they needed to be more flexible and understanding. After a few days of gradually softening the cancellation policy, they told travellers they would get a full refund if they chose not to travel. No questions, no strings attached. "George bet the business on what he decided to do," claims Paul Christopher. "Nobody else

September 12 marked the single busiest day of the year, with more trips and travellers on the road than ever before

was doing what he was doing. But he saw it as an opportunity to do the right thing and felt, ultimately, that the travellers would reward B&R with their loyalty." Thankfully, they did. The remaining trips that season ran at half capacity or better, and many who did not travel simply rebooked for the following year. B&R's suppliers also cooperated, graciously returning pre-paid deposits they technically had the right to keep.

The company had survived its biggest storm, but the clouds still hung low. "It felt as though the world had changed in some fundamental way," reflects Norm. "The business was in the process of figuring out how to change and adapt. It was a tough couple of years." Reacting to the generally diminished appetite for travel, B&R reduced the number of trips and destinations for the following year and introduced the Peace of Mind Protection Plan (or POMPP), a self-insured policy designed to ease travellers' concerns about committing to a trip.

While those measures helped to streamline operations and encourage sales, a new issue was emerging – a number of Americans were suddenly not so keen on France. President George W. Bush was readying for an invasion of Iraq, and the French had made it clear they would not be participating. The ensuing anti-French sentiment led to Freedom Fries and several delicate phone conversations for

"Are you f@*#ing
You guys don't
There's competi

B&R's travel advisers. Kelly remembers the words of one traveller: "I don't want to go anywhere right now because I'm scared. Next year I want to go somewhere I'm going to feel safe as an American, and also where I'm supporting a country that has supported us." The fading enthusiasm for all things French was bad for business. Before 9/11, France had been a B&R traveller favourite, accounting for nearly half of all the trips.

Not only was the company's prized horse hobbled but the field of competitors was closing in. For years B&R had downplayed the threat from imitators, supremely confident that a strong brand and superior trips would be enough to guarantee success. The blinders were summarily removed at a meeting with the company's Advisory Board, which had been formed in the late nineties and met with the owners and the management team a couple of times a year. After a manager innocently remarked that "B&R didn't really *have* any competition," Erik Blachford, freshly appointed CEO of Expedia and a member of the board, slammed his fist on the table: "Are you f@*#ing kidding me?" he charged. "You guys don't have a clue. There's competition everywhere!" And so there was.

"We had our heads far in the clouds," admits George. B&R had been so busy planning trips to cool new destinations, seeking out the

kidding me?
have a clue.
tion everywhere!"

most special events, and collecting the finest hotels that they failed to realize they'd essentially become a research and development department for their competitors. Suddenly, every biking and walking company seemed to be saying the same thing, staying at the same hotels, and booking tables at the same restaurants. Delivering an amazing trip experience is one thing, but explaining what makes it unique is a whole other challenge. B&R was struggling to communicate its edge and hold on to its slice of the premium travel pie.

In previous eras there had always been a fairly clear sense of who was running the show on a day-to-day basis. Martha, Sidney, and George had steered the business through the sixties and seventies. Then it was George, Tom Hamilton, and, for a few years, Danny Legault in the eighties and early nineties. Michael Liss, enabled by George and massively supported by a host of other people, dominated the balance of the nineties. Gil Roberts pulled the trigger on the new millennium – leaving just a couple of months before 9/11. For a few years thereafter, George wasn't entirely certain what kind of leadership he wanted for the company.

He was partly of the mind that a seasoned outsider was needed – someone who could navigate the complex and competitive new environment. But the hunt for a "creative business dude," as George

PREVIOUS
*Don't forget to
look over your
shoulder in the
Italian Lake
District*

ABOVE
*The Butterfields,
dusty but happy
on safari in
Tanzania*

puts it, bore little fruit. "I was looking for somebody, but deep down I knew I wasn't ready to let go," he admits.

While the external search for a saviour continued, so did life within the walls of B&R. To keep the business running smoothly, George formed a "steering committee," which soon evolved into a four-person management team known as PINC (so named for its members, Paul Christopher, Ian Newall, Norm Howe, and Courtenay Vuchnich). It might not have been the sort of leadership structure George was used to (as Chris Tabbitt comments, "George liked to have one guy he could go off to lunch with and jam on ideas"), but it proved a good solution for the turbulent years immediately following 9/11. The four communicated well with one another and capably managed their corners of the business. Paul held the numbers together, Ian kept operations tight, Norm filled the role of quasi-general manager, and Courtenay tested new marketing ideas.

In time, however, it was apparent that PINC wasn't an ideal long-term solution for anyone. George was getting restless. The business had stabilized somewhat, but the vision was fragmented, or at the very least murky. Viva Dolan, the design agency that had been responsible for creating B&R's marketing materials for nearly ten years (winning over 300 design awards in the process), felt they

BUTTERFIELD **B**

could no longer "protect the B&R premium," and in 2003 parted ways. That same year a handful of long-time staff decided it was time to move on, as did Norm. "We were going through another restructuring," he says, "and I had exhausted my potential in the role. The only thing left was to run the place – and that's what I wanted to do. George and I discussed it, but he concluded he wasn't ready to hand me the keys."

Soon to be turning sixty-five, George was beginning to think seriously about succession. He didn't yet have a plan. Son David Butterfield had worked on and off for B&R for many years, first as a bike mechanic, then as a guide on student and adult trips, later as a trip planner and route manager for a variety of countries (including Mexico, Argentina, Brazil, Chile, Austria, and Spain), and in 1997–98 as B&R's "Man in Marrakech," running the Morocco program. But as he grew older, he discovered winemaking, fell in love with France (and his now wife, Juliette), and decided to develop his own venture, Butterfield Wine. Daughter Nathalie Butterfield followed a different but similarly independent path. She too did some guiding and seasonal work for B&R, but after practising law for a few years, she decided to blaze her own trail as an entrepreneur and started a sustainable textile goods company called Fluf. "David and I have gone off to start our

own businesses because our parents made it look so doable and so much fun," she says.

As for Luc Robinson, the son of Sidney and Linda Robinson (she had been a French teacher and B&R guide in the late seventies before she went to law school and began practising with Osler, Hoskin & Harcourt LLP), he too was out of the running. Notwithstanding his keen intellect, relative maturity, and experience as a traveller on B&R family trips, he was not yet old enough to shave.

For George, it was a slow realization that none of the children he, Martha, and Sidney had among them would be involved in B&R in quite the way he had dreamed. "He just wanted so badly to see a succession in the family," says David. Not only is multi-generational business in his blood (the Bermuda food-importing company started by his grandfather is now in the hands of the fourth generation) but George is hard-wired to take the long view. Above all else, he's a family man.

To celebrate Christmas 2003 the Butterfields (George and Martha, David and Juliette, Nathalie and her boyfriend, Benson Cowan) joined B&R's inaugural Antarctica Expedition aboard the brand-new, 106-passenger *Orion*. Like other Expedition trips, the journey was an uncommon blend of remote access, unlikely luxury, and moderate physical activity. After setting sail from Ushuaia, the ship

crossed the infamously choppy Drake Passage and spent the next ten days exploring the numbingly beautiful Antarctic Peninsula. There were daily shore excursions to see wildlife and explore on foot, and ample time, in the words of the brochure, to "drink 12-year-old scotch over 1000-year-old ice" in the lounge. It was here that George got to know his future son-in-law.

"He kept talking about us working together," recalls Benson, "but the only way that was going to happen was if he killed someone and needed a criminal defence attorney." George wasn't looking for legal representation, but he appreciated Benson's sharp mind and gradually got the idea that a family succession was in the cards after all. And so the wooing began. "I thought he was crazy because I didn't have any experience in the business whatsoever," continues Benson. "But part of me was saying, 'When in your life is anyone ever going to offer you a chance to run the business and expand your horizons? You'd be an idiot to turn it down.'"

In February 2004 Nathalie and Benson were married in a surprise wedding at George and Martha's house (the guests were told it was an engagement party). By May, Benson was out of law and into B&R. With the complete and enthusiastic support of George and Martha, his initial role was to lead the Bespoke planning team that was responsible for B&R's private trips – the fastest-growing part of the

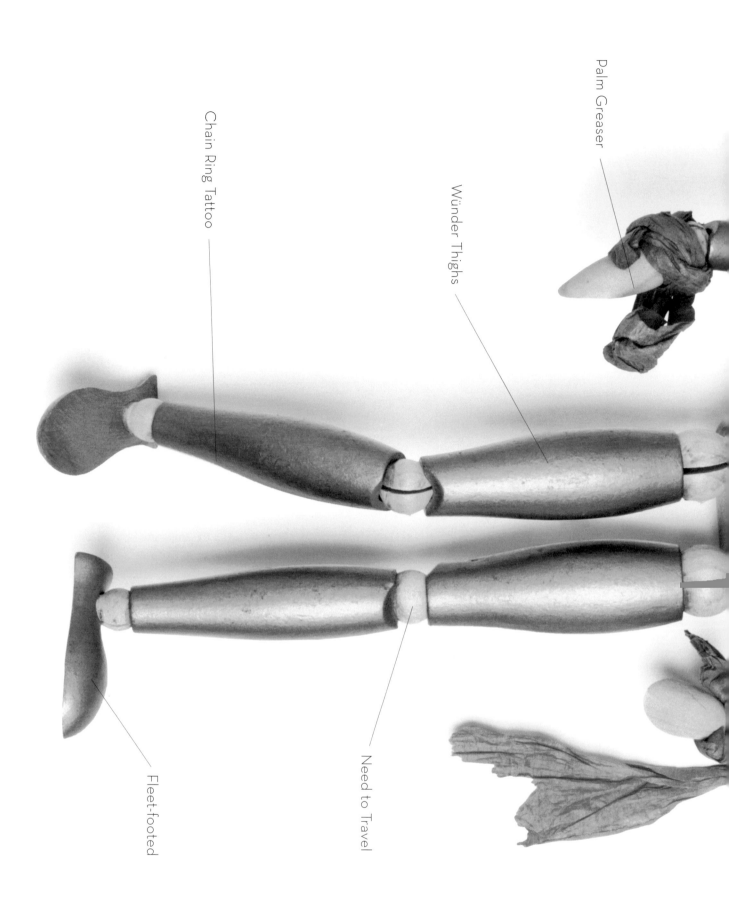

Palm Greaser

Wünder Thighs

Chain Ring Tattoo

Fleet-footed

Need to Travel

Meet a Sidney

At the end of each guiding season, Sidney awards are handed out to B&R guides who have demonstrated extraordinary creativity, leadership, resourcefulness, and/or patience. Here's what it take to win a Sidney.

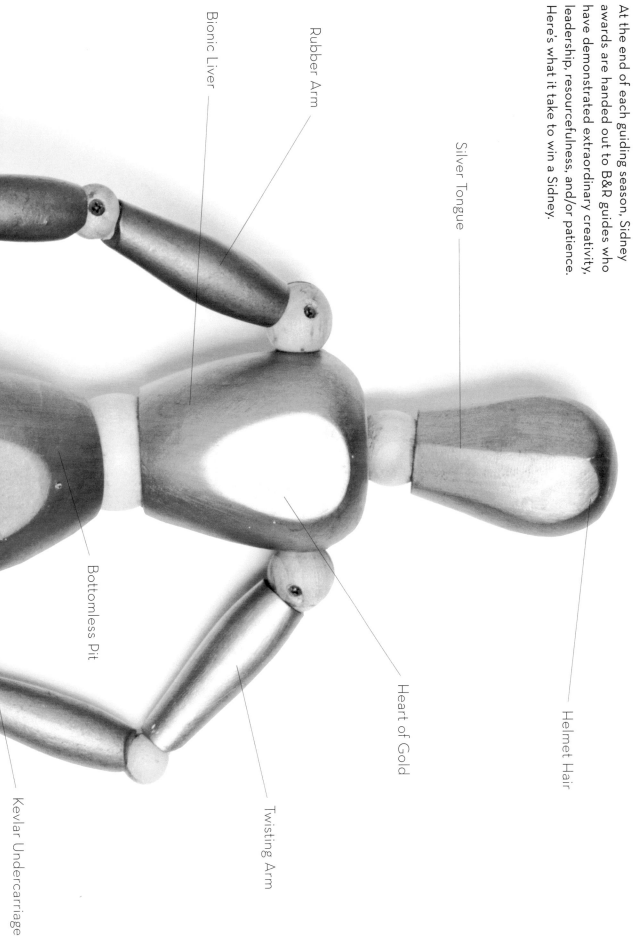

Silver Tongue

Bionic Liver

Rubber Arm

Bottomless Pit

Heart of Gold

Helmet Hair

Twisting Arm

Kevlar Undercarriage

business. It didn't take a genius to see what was going on. After several years of searching, George had found a solution that he felt was the right one. He was ready to take a step back and give Benson all the rope he wanted.

When Benson officially took the wheel as managing director in mid-2005, there was a renewed sense of optimism at B&R, relief even, that someone was finally in charge – and, critically, empowered. Benson brought with him a fresh perspective on what B&R could do, what the business could be. Encouraged at one of the Advisory Board meetings to "build his own team," Benson took the suggestion to heart and quickly set about restructuring the staff in his vision. Whereas B&R had long promoted from within the organization (guides became regional directors became sales managers), there was now a conscious move to hire outsiders – professionals from diverse non-travel backgrounds. "It was as though he had a chess game going on," says Trish Kaliciak, who joined the marketing team shortly before Benson's arrival. "He was very specific about who he wanted." If they had the right skills, he reckoned, they could learn to understand the brand.

For many employees who had been with B&R for years, developing new skills while living the brand, the shift in leadership approach

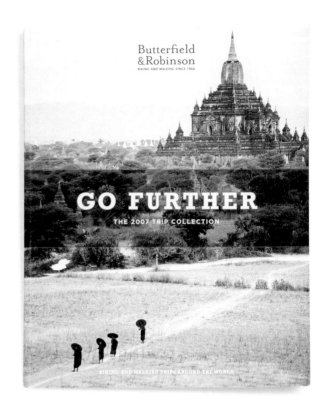

ABOVE
Benson and George enjoy a bière pression post bike ride

BELOW
Laura Finch brings out a basket of goodies

was jarring. Over the next few years a number of the old guard left or got squeezed out. Vicky Bake, Nicky Speakman, Kelly McKinney, Ian Newall, Chris Tabbitt, and Muriel Truter – all were gone by 2007.

As the door revolved, B&R's core business of adult biking and walking trips continued to roll along at a decent pace. Traveller numbers held steady, and new people emerged to fill the key roles. Laura Finch, a long-time B&R guide and employee, became the guide coordinator – ensuring that the right kind of people were hired for the critical task of leading stellar trips. Grant Gordon, a writer and branding savant, became the new messenger of the message. To this day Grant and his agency, Key Gordon Communications, play a huge role in creating B&R's brochures and steering the print and digital voice of B&R.

Thanks in part to Benson's decision to increase prices to reflect higher costs, the bottom line was healthy. With the breathing room afforded by economic and brand momentum, Benson focused the business on areas where he saw the greatest demand and potential. He doubled the size of the marketing team, channelled significant resources into developing a website that would feature B&R's hand-picked hotel collection, and spent huge sums upgrading the company's customer service platform and reservation system.

ABOVE LEFT
*An informal
meeting in the
expanded
Toronto office*

ABOVE RIGHT
*Tyler Dillon
(middle) and
travellers loping
along the Silk
Road*

With all the additional staff on Bond Street, the office had to expand. Benson had an impressive staircase built to connect B&R's third-floor space with the newly leased floor above. George, who wasn't spending as much time at the office, was moved upstairs, and Benson settled into his former digs beside the meeting room. The dream was big, and the budgets were even bigger. But that was okay – business was pretty good and, looking ahead into late 2007, it seemed to be getting better still.

Then, in January 2008, as the storm clouds began to gather in the world's financial markets, the air didn't smell as sweet in B&R's office either. Bookings slowed down. "You could tell George knew something was wrong," says Chris Mark, a trip planner in the Toronto office.

Nothing restores a weary spirit like travel, however, so in the early spring George and Benson decided to hit the road – the Silk Road, in fact. For a couple of years B&R had been running adventure trips that followed a section of the Far East's most famous path through China. The extreme geography and exotic culture had struck a chord with seasoned travellers, so B&R decided to reach further into the unknown and research possible routes in Uzbekistan. George and Benson also saw their get-away as a cool opportunity to involve the

media and earn some press for B&R. They would join a scheduled B&R Silk Road trip and then continue on to Uzbekistan with a magazine writer, freelance photographer, and Tyler Dillon, the B&R guide.

The day before the trip was due to begin, Tyler got an email from George saying that he and Benson would be arriving a day late – maybe two. There was stuff going on in Toronto. By day three they still weren't there, and the journey needed to continue. Tyler flew with the group from Xi'an (home of the terracotta warriors) to Dunhuang, an ancient frontier town in northwest China on the edge of the Taklamakan Desert – a forbidding land whose name loosely translates from Uyghur as "once you go in, you won't come out." It was here that the South and North Silk Roads came together or went their separate ways, depending on one's perspective.

Sitting on a rooftop, overlooking the sand dunes that evening, Tyler and the B&R travellers talked about the strange day it had been. Minutes after landing in Dunhuang they'd learned about a massive earthquake that had struck the province of Sichuan, near the city of Chengdu, while they were in the air – mercifully more than 2,000 kilometres, or 1,200 miles, away. Tens of thousands had lost their lives. Just as the group was sitting down for dinner, Tyler's phone rang. It was George. He was still in Canada, and he wouldn't be

The Active Activist

Under normal circumstances it would have been disappointing that only one person attended the screening of Martha's documentary, *Exposure: Environmental Links to Breast Cancer*, when it was featured at the New York Independent Film Festival in 2001. But it wasn't much of a surprise. Not even Martha was able to attend. Five days before, on September 11, the World Trade Center had been attacked – and the city was reeling. Only Michael Liss was in the theatre that evening. He'd managed to drive back to New York the day before and, at Martha's request, was on hand to introduce the film Martha had written and co-produced.

Fortunately, the award-winning documentary, narrated by Olivia Newton-John, had been enthusiastically received at numerous film festivals and earlier screenings, including at the United Nations in New York and the Parliament Buildings in Ottawa.

For Martha, the film was an opportunity to do what she does best – speak up. Raising awareness of important issues, questioning the status quo, furthering the lives of women and girls, and defending the underdog are central to her character and a key part of her contribution to B&R. "Martha has always been the social conscience of the business – always promoting social justice and things like that," says Norm Howe. "George has become more aligned with that as time has gone on." Like a good mother, Martha has nurtured B&R's sense of equality and fairness. She's helped to keep the company humble and human.

coming to China. It was a difficult time for him and the family: Benson was leaving B&R. George asked Tyler to apologize to the group; he was so sorry not to be joining them for the adventure. And then he hung up the phone.

The following day George called the doctor – not a *doctor* doctor but Peter Tolnai, a member of B&R's Advisory Board and a long-time friend and confidante. After taking his first B&R trip to the Loire Valley in 1985, Peter had written George a letter with his thoughts on B&R's product and service. His pragmatic perspective and venture capital background impressed George and, before long, Peter was flying back and forth to Bermuda, helping the food-importing company with its complicated acquisition of a competitor. Peter was in his element. "Maybe it's a bad character trait of mine, but I like a mess," he admits. "I'm attracted to difficult situations where I can do what nobody else will do. I'm like an emergency doctor for companies."

Walking into B&R in May 2008, Peter found a messy operational situation indeed. Benson's sudden departure had sent a wave through the company, and, as the world's financial situation became ever more precarious, consumer confidence fell too. People weren't sure that spending money on a luxury vacation was a good idea, at least

"It was like a freight train coming toward us. All the good stuff we were doing to manage the business got dwarfed by the foreign exchange losses"

not then. After the collapse of Lehman Brothers in mid-September, things worsened dramatically. "It's hard to describe the free fall, it was unbelievable," says Peter. Plummeting traveller numbers were one issue, but bloated overheads became an even bigger problem. B&R had been optimistically building for significant growth, and that was definitely not going to happen. Tougher still was getting caught on the wrong side of a currency hedge. "It was like a freight train coming toward us," Peter winces. "All the good stuff we were doing to manage the business got dwarfed by the foreign exchange losses."

The most painful loss of all, however, was saying goodbye to so many employees. Robin Wark, B&R's director of human resources, recalls what happened: "We took three cracks at restructuring the business. Just when we thought we had it right, we realized we needed to let more people go." Over a fourteen-month period, B&R reduced its staff by nearly half. Peter did what had to be done to save the patient, but it wasn't fun for anybody. "Every time I had trouble logging into my computer I thought I'd lost my job," says Chris Mark, whose wife (B&R alumna Meredith Frye) had just given birth to their third child. For George, whom Martha claims "sleeps like a baby, even when the world is coming to an end," the situation had him tossing and turning at night. Some companies measure their health by numbers. At B&R it's happy people that count.

Whenever B&R had faced a crisis (or an opportunity) in the past, George had always returned to his maxim: "It's all about leading great trips." Peter had done an extraordinary job of bringing the business back to a functional and realistic size. But as George started thinking about how to rehabilitate the spirit of B&R, he looked deep within the organization. Who would have an understanding of guiding and trip planning as well as the necessary chops and character to lead the company? At the top of his list was Erik Blachford.

Long part of the B&R family, Erik had been involved with the business, on and off, for twenty-five years – as a traveller, guide, researcher, route manager, and Advisory Board member. He'd become good friends with George and Martha, and he'd proven himself a smart, responsible, fun, and very creative guy. That last quality was especially important for George: for him, few things contribute more to the magic of a trip than creativity.

Legendary around B&R was the stunt Erik pulled in 1993 during a Burgundy trip he guided. During dinner he proposed to award a magnum of Puligny-Montrachet Premier Cru (the sort of wine that brings people to tears) to anyone who would spend the night in a genuine *cave à vin* (wine cellar) under the medieval streets of Beaune. A young couple tentatively raised their hands. After post-dinner drinks at Pickwick's Pub, Erik escorted the anxious pair (and some curious hangers-on) to their quarters for the night.

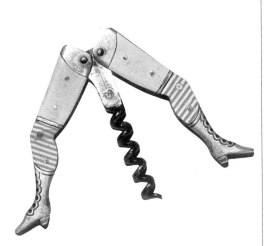

Once everyone's eyes adjusted to the romantic candlelight, they could see it wasn't going to be such an arduous sleep after all. A proper bedroom had been set up with white linen sheets on an antique bed, side tables, and a Persian rug. "Damn, I *knew* we should have done it," muttered a disappointed traveller. The brave volunteers got their prized bottle and emerged the next morning – engaged. Notwithstanding a pissed-off cellar owner (alas, the *cave* had no *toilette*), it was a perfect piece of B&R theatre.

As luck would have it, Erik had some time on his hands when George called him that summer of 2009. He was no longer with Expedia and was not yet working full-time on a new project. "I told George I would sign up to help for a while," recalls Erik, "and if it worked out, I'd buy in." Unusually for George, he put some equity on the table. He totally trusted Erik and wanted a long-term commitment. After initially exploring the idea of moving the company to San Francisco, where Erik lived with his wife and children, they decided that B&R's home should stay in Toronto.

With that, Erik began commuting to Toronto every second week. The office vibe quickly improved. Not only was he well regarded for his experience inside and outside B&R but his presence was a sign that the company had turned the corner. The cuts were over, and B&R was ready to shift from survival mode to strategic planning. Erik's charisma re-booted office morale and put company culture

"I felt there was unfinished business, and I felt that B&R was my spiritual home"

back at centre stage. He empowered guides and younger staff to step into new roles and kept B&R focused on numbers and measurement. Yes, it had to be fun, but it also had to be a viable and vibrant business.

The route to rebuilding was hard work and full of challenges. "Erik had a five-thousand-mile problem," says George. "He lived in San Francisco, and the business was in Toronto." The massive commute was crushing him and, by late 2010, Erik knew he needed to modify the game plan. It turned out that Norm Howe was at loose ends, having recently sold a travel business he'd been involved with since leaving B&R in 2003. The wheels turned quickly and, by January 2011, Norm was back at B&R, ready to run the daily operation under Erik as president and CEO. "I felt there was unfinished business, and I felt that B&R was my spiritual home," Norm says.

B&R's leadership was back on solid ground, but the economy was still limping along. "We looked back to see what the rebound was like after the Gulf War in 1992 and post-9/11," reflects Erik. "Those were pretty fast bounces. One tough season, and you were back in business. I think we all thought the same thing was going to happen after the 2008 financial meltdown, but it didn't. It was tough." Erik was baffled, George was tired, and everyone (Martha and Sidney included) was getting tired of pumping money into the business.

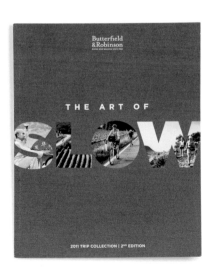

"We all lost faith," admits Martha, "and we didn't want B&R to die inch by inch."

"In early 2012 we started talking to some guys who'd been sniffing around for years to buy us," recalls Norm. Two billionaires, each with a different angle for wanting to buy the company, were serious. One of them sent his "business drones," as David Butterfield labelled them, to 70 Bond Street to do their due diligence discreetly. A few weeks later, Erik and George flew to the States for serious negotiations.

Remembering the moment, George closes his eyes and shakes his head. "I asked them what time we should meet for dinner, and they said, 'Does 5:00 pm suit you? When we sat down I asked if they'd like some wine, and they said, 'No thanks, we don't drink.'" Erik and George ordered a bottle anyway, and by 6:30 dinner was over. "Clearly this wasn't a perfect meshing of cultures," says Erik. But back in Toronto a few days later, when a firm offer to purchase arrived, all of B&R's shareholders agreed to move the deal forward and a letter of intent was signed.

Toronto's Jarvis Street links the quiet, green neighbourhood of Rosedale to the mostly grey and glass downtown core of the city to the south. Though it's five lanes wide (three in the direction of rush-hour traffic, two the other way), things tend to move slowly. On the morning the sale of B&R was due to close, David Butterfield was back in town for the annual general meeting. He and George had time to chat as their car crawled down Jarvis toward the B&R office. David wasn't sure that selling B&R was a great idea after all. He kept thinking about his grandfather (George's dad, Dudley) who died at ninety-one with a cigar in one hand and a martini in the other. What would George do without B&R in his life? The business was his centre of gravity – it fed his soul. He needed it for his health, figured David. He shared his views with George and reminded him that,

PREVIOUS
*Riding the line
on the Dalmatian
Coast*

ABOVE
*Head first on a
By Sea trip*

surely, the worst was behind them. The financial upside to the sale wasn't compelling, and David was concerned about the potential emotional downside – heart-wrenching regret.

Eventually, they arrived at 70 Bond Street. George got out of the car and made his way to the front door, but not before David offered a final shot: "Remember what we discussed, Dad. Don't sell the business."

As George made his way slowly up the creaky stairs, he digested the conversation from the car. And he remembered a comment that Roger Martin, his friend and member of the Advisory Board, had made a few days earlier. "What will happen if the acquisition fails and the new buyers sell B&R for parts? How will you feel?" By the time George reached his office, now back to its original spot on the third floor, he knew exactly how he felt.

But before he could do anything, the phone rang. It was Erik. He was calling to explain to George, at length, all the reasons he'd decided B&R should *not* sell. After listening quietly, George told Erik he'd already come to the same conclusion. "Then why did you make me talk for twenty minutes?" asked Erik. They both laughed.

At 4:00 pm that day George called an impromptu Huddle in the Toronto office. He shared the big news that B&R was not being sold after all. Faces went blank. Apart from a couple of the managers, no one knew it had been for sale in the first place. "So it was a bit of a shock," says Norm.

The Fundamentals

There's a difference between getting older and growing up. At fifty, the culture of B&R still has a twinkle in its eye and a youthful skip in its step. A dig through the archive makes it easy to see why.

Growth through Innovation

For more than five decades George, Martha, and Sidney have been serious about keeping things silly.

Assets & Liabilities

When it comes to B&R party wear, some outfits and accoutrements are more valuable currency than others.

Fake moustache, fake teeth, terry cloth jumpsuit, fishnet stockings (worn by a man), cowboy hat, any hat, vintage ball gown, wedding dress, plumage, papal garb, eye patch, kimono, kilt.

Blue dress shirt, haute couture ball gown, rep tie, briefcase, mink stole, lace-up brogues, suspenders, fishnet stockings (worn by a woman), pocket watch, pantsuit.

George 'DD' Butterfield learns the ropes from his mentor Dick Gibb

Martha aces the talent show aboard the Leonardo da Vinci on the first trip

*Not man
people k
George
to wear*

Sorry, I thought you said 'Chef Operating Officer'

Rabid enthusiasm at a holiday staff party

George, Linda, Martha, and Sidney masquerading as adults

Training family in corporat value sy

All the Trimmings

It's not just what you wear, but how you wear it. Of the many ways to dress for dinner, these are the most (and least) popular.

■ Cross-dressing
≡ Undressing
■ Power dressing
≡ Thousand Island dressing

89%

Wigging out

Percentage of people wearing wigs at a typical B&R event.

Upcycling a plastic bag for Mardi Gras

Preaching to the converted

Jaunty George and his long-time friend Stan Macfarlane

There's no reason to be uncomfortable in the red

Putting some "arghh" in B&R

Confucius says 'Slow down, you move too fast'

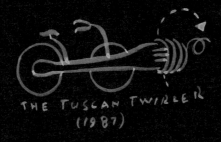

THE TUSCAN TWIRLER
(1987)

"I like nonsense; it wakes up the brain cells."

DR. SEUSS

6

2012
-
2015

Happy in the Saddle

Ponte degli Scalzi

"I began to believe in myself and in the brand again," George says candidly. By doubling down and renewing his commitment to the business, he breathed a huge gust of optimism into B&R"

There are a lot of good reasons why jumping into a canal in Venice, Italy, is a bad idea. To name but one – the romantic waterways, washed by the tides and the sea, also function as an enormous open-air sewer system. Yet, while guiding a B&R trip on a stifling August day in 1967, George decided that a swim in one of the murky canals would be a terrific way to beat the heat. Leaping from a bridge into the opaque green water below, the smile on his face was enough to convince the student travellers that it was a brilliant idea. One by one they followed suit. "It was like watching lemmings on that bridge," recalls Martha. "Lemmings who got back out of the water and jumped in again – over and over."

That's the genius of George. His enthusiasm and easy charm make him the sort of person you want to follow – even when it's not initially clear where or why. Sidney puts it plainly: "People like him, they trust him, and he inspires confidence." More than sixty years of friendship lend some credibility to his take on things. But even if you've known George for only sixty seconds, it's obvious he's got some social superpowers. There's that sixth sense for hosting (given the option, he will always choose a round dining table to facilitate conversation) and a casual relentlessness for sharing experiences and discoveries. And, of course, the graciousness. "He doesn't make anybody feel uncomfortable," says Richard Meech, the guide behind the adult trips. "No matter who he meets, he relates to them as an equal."

SLOW DOWN TO SEE THE WORLD 2013

Butterfield & Robinson

It's a good thing George is a remarkable leader. B&R, having come close to being sold in the winter of 2012, clearly needed a dose of George's energy as much as he needed the company. Nearly a decade of turbulence had slowly drained the wind from its sails. "I began to believe in myself and in the brand again," George says candidly. By doubling down and renewing his commitment to the business, he breathed a huge gust of optimism into B&R. Listening to George speak from the heart at the Huddle that afternoon reminded everyone why they loved working at B&R – and refreshed their own enthusiasm. "It made everyone walk a little taller and want to do their jobs even better," remarks Trish Kaliciak.

While it may have seemed that George was encouraging another leap into the unknown, his faith in the business was well founded. As usual, his gut instinct was based on something real – heaps of experience, careful observation, and sound judgement. After a few painful years of trimming and toning, B&R was finally the right size and shape for the road ahead. Succumbing to the challenge of trying to run a company far from home, Erik Blachford decided to leave B&R shortly after the almost-sale. In his wake was a highly capable team of managers led by Norm Howe, who happily filled the role of CEO. Norm had gained a lot of sales and operational experience during his

first stint at B&R (1997–2003), but being co-owner of another respected Canadian travel company for the ensuing seven years rounded out his perspective and skill as a leader. "I got to understand how hard the challenges of being an entrepreneur are," he concedes. "You can't appreciate it until you're involved." The new and improved Norm was ready to take the helm.

In short order, B&R was once again financially healthy and emotionally happy. The culture was nourishing itself, and innovation was back at centre stage. Electric bikes were introduced as an option for travellers wanting to enjoy hilly regions such as Tuscany without incurring the full brunt (and grunt) of the climbs. And the Bistro line of trips was launched as a less expensive alternative to the classic biking and walking trips. They included all the character and originality travellers had come to expect from B&R, but with somewhat less fluffy towels.

Private trips, which accounted for less than 10 percent of the business in 2000, rocketed to more than half of the total – as much a reflection of travellers' growing desire for flexibility as B&R's enthusiasm for crafting uniqueness. Evolving to meet the various shades of interest in tailored travel, B&R offered everything from

Private trips, which accounted for less than 10 percent of the business in 2000, rocketed to more than half of the total

"Martha pushes him to think of issues he might not have considered. I know that when they make big decisions they make them together"

mildly modified existing itineraries to wildly creative bespoke trips built completely from scratch. It was even possible to travel on a customized independent adventure without a B&R guide – something unimaginable a few years before. "Norm quickly untied a lot of the product rules we'd been following," says Kathy Stewart, a twenty-year trip-planning veteran of B&R. "It was really exciting and liberating. We had to change and evolve – and we hadn't been doing that for a while."

In a sense B&R wasn't doing anything new at all. It was simply returning to its roots – focusing on the talent and expertise of its people and letting the trips take whatever form best captured the spirit of the day. What had changed was George's relationship with the day-to-day leadership of the company. From the beginning he had struggled to find the right balance between the art and science of running the business. At various times in the past the pendulum had disruptively swung too far one way or the other. "I think he finally learned how to let go and get good people in there to do the work better than he does," comments Richard, "and yet maintain his position as the founder and *éminence grise*."

There's a question that's floated around the company for almost as long as there's been a B&R: "What would George do?" Simultaneously specific and abstract, it's a simple way to measure an idea or a situation against the personality that has become the brand. While George has been the face of B&R ("the magician keeping the wave going," as marketing guru Michael Liss suggests) for almost fifty years, he's quick to point out that the company's success is due to

the enormous effort of many. The other thing George would clarify is that he'd rarely do anything of significance without first turning to Martha for her input. "She pushes him to think of issues he might not have considered," says their daughter, Nathalie. "I know that when they make big decisions they make them together."

In any case, "What would George do?" is indeed the question – one that triggers a few more. How is it that B&R has survived for so many years? What makes the culture of the company so special? What should B&R do next? The answers are hidden in plain sight, woven into the reality of what George, Martha, and Sidney have done right from day one.

First and foremost, George has created a space where interesting things can happen – a kingdom where creativity is king, curiosity is queen, and everyone is welcome to eat, drink, and be merry. "It was as though he was inventing a world of travel. An escape from a version

Flying the Coop

You don't have to dig very deep in the travel industry to find B&R alumni. Dozens and dozens of former guides have left B&R over the years to start their own hotels, tour operators, consultancies, and trip-planning companies. For so many young people, fresh out of university and new to the real world, B&R was a place to pursue their true passions, learn some practical skills, and gain confidence – a refinishing school of sorts. "There just wasn't enough room for most of them to stay," says David Young. "They almost got too much of that B&R spirit – 'Go, do your own thing.'"

Yet B&R never resented its staff soaking up all that knowledge and experience, only to leave to start potentially competitive businesses. "Everybody was giving me advice to be a lot tougher and not so casual about it," says George. "But I didn't buy it. I thought if people come here and do great work, but we don't have jobs to keep them all or they want different challenges, why shouldn't they be allowed to go off and do their own thing?" He has always felt that businesses need to breathe people out as comfortably as they breathe them in.

That's not to say there haven't been a few unsettling departures. On more than one occasion guides have waltzed off with client lists plucked

of adulthood that was just so dry, so boring," says the writer David Young, who has remained close with George and Martha since they first hired him to be a *baggagiste* on a student trip almost five decades ago. In the same way that a B&R trip has always been about orchestrating an experience so that the unexpected has a place to happen, George has nurtured an environment where people feel excited and comfortable enough to be their most engaging and fun selves. For anyone who values quality over quantity, B&R is a refreshing place to be – way more about lifestyle than business.

Building a great stage is one thing, but picking the right actors is another. George has excelled with that. "He has an incredible ability to spot and unlock talent," says Norm. "He's always been in love with creativity and creative people, but to actually realize that creativity, see it and liberate it, is an unusual thing." At B&R there's been a willingness to look past someone's proven ability and focus on their potential ability. Time and again guides have been plucked from obscurity and handed roles and responsibilities light years beyond their apparent expertise. He hasn't always hit the mark, but way more often than not his belief in people has been enough to ensure their success.

"The trust that he placed in people and the confidence he gave them to go off and figure it out was remarkable," says Vicky Bake, who

unscrupulously from the filing cabinet or the database. And it's hard to forget the story of the guide who handed out business cards for his new tour company while guiding a B&R trip – the bike mechanics found several of the cards in the handlebar bags when they sorted out equipment after the trip.

George also recognizes that B&R didn't invent the wheel. Just as he, Martha, and Sidney borrowed the idea of exploring Europe by bicycle from Gibb-Macfarlane, others have emulated the B&R approach. As the French-Swiss filmmaker Jean-Luc Godard once said, "It's not where you take things from – it's where you take them to."

After fifty years of putting their unique spin on travel, B&R was thrilled to be named the "World's Best Tour Operator" by readers of *Travel & Leisure* magazine in July 2015. It's hard to beat an original.

decades ago jetted off to Spain at short notice to figure out a new trip. David Young explains it another way: "George wanted people who would go out to the end of the rope but not do something stupid." "He's really a firm believer in allowing people to grow and develop themselves," adds Peter Tolnai.

Just as important, George has never been daunted by failure. "In most companies," comments Roger Martin, the author of several business books and articles, "new ideas get subjected to standards of proof that either neuter them completely or prevent them from happening. At B&R, if you come forward with a plausible idea that won't sink the ship, even if it fails completely, then you have a pretty good chance to give it a whirl." By taking the long view, George has never fussed too much about the inevitable bumps and dips along the way. You win some, you lose some. "He has the ability to roll with things to a much greater degree than most of us," muses Richard.

Above all else, George has safeguarded an unconventional spark – a mindset that puts people and experiences ahead of profits. Anytime B&R has lost its way, he's always brought the focus back to the trip. If people are deliriously happy, he figures, everything else will take care of itself. And really, how can you not enjoy slowing down to see the world?

ABOVE
George finding his way

Whenever George is in Beaune he always finds time to hop on a bike. It's where he most likes to be – and the reason why Butterfield & Robinson exists. Yes, it's a business, but far more than that it's simply a way to live a good life. When you allow yourself the time to enjoy things and get a little exercise, they are almost always more fun. You see more, smell more, hear more, and connect with people more. You can eat and drink more while you understand and appreciate where you are.

George's favourite bike route follows the narrow roads that connect the town of Beaune with the low-lying winemaking village of Pommard and the hamlets of Meloisey and Nantoux, far up the slopes of the Hautes Côtes. The ride begins bumpily, across cobbled streets, as you make your way through the centre of Beaune. You roll past the *boulangerie* (perhaps stopping to grab a *pain au chocolat* in case of emergency), weave around the old lady returning from the market with a heavy straw bag stuffed with fruit and vegetables, and a few minutes later you're free – embraced by the gorgeous countryside.

"The vines are all around you and the hills are steep enough to make you work," says George. "But they're manageable, and you feel like you've climbed a mountain. Once you're at the top you know you've earned your way down. It doesn't get any better."

George's 8½ Rules of Slow

1 Sniff out your own corner. Instead of scrapping over the same bone as all the other dogs, go find your own.

2 It's okay to be a little crazy. There should be no lid on creativity. Many of our best ideas initially seemed ridiculous.

3 Throw lots of spaghetti. The more things you try, the better the chances that you will find something that sticks.

4 Jettison the jargon – it won't save you. Use your own words. Original language is refreshing and stands out.

5 Listen to your gut. More often than not your well-honed instincts will trump the best-laid plans.

6 Listen to the numbers too. Take in more money than you spend. (An acknowledgement: we still have not learned how to do this every year, but when we do, it's way more fun.)

7 Don't hold back. Share everything with your staff: business strategies, financials, profits, and most of all, the special times.

8 Never stop caring about whatever it is that you care about. If you do stop, it's time to go find something new.

8½ Start something and see where it goes...

Ithaka

C. P. CAVAFY

As you set out for Ithaka
hope your road is a long one,
full of adventure, full of discovery.
Laistrygonians, Cyclops,
angry Poseidon - don't be afraid of them:
you'll never find things like that on your way
as long as you keep your thoughts raised high,
as long as a rare excitement
stirs your spirit and your body.
Laistrygonians, Cyclops,
wild Poseidon - you won't encounter them
unless you bring them along inside your soul,
unless your soul sets them up in front of you.

Hope your road is a long one.
May there be many summer mornings when,
with what pleasure, what joy,
you enter harbors you're seeing for the first time;
may you stop at Phoenician trading stations
to buy fine things,
mother of pearl and coral, amber and ebony,
sensual perfume of every kind -
as many sensual perfumes as you can;
and may you visit many Egyptian cities
to learn and go on learning from their scholars.

Keep Ithaka always in your mind.
Arriving there is what you're destined for.
But don't hurry the journey at all.
Better if it lasts for years,
so you're old by the time you reach the island,
wealthy with all you've gained on the way,
not expecting Ithaka to make you rich.

Ithaka gave you the marvelous journey.
Without her you wouldn't have set out.
She has nothing left to give you now.

And if you find her poor, Ithaka won't have fooled you.
Wise as you will have become, so full of experience,
you'll have understood by then what these Ithakas mean.

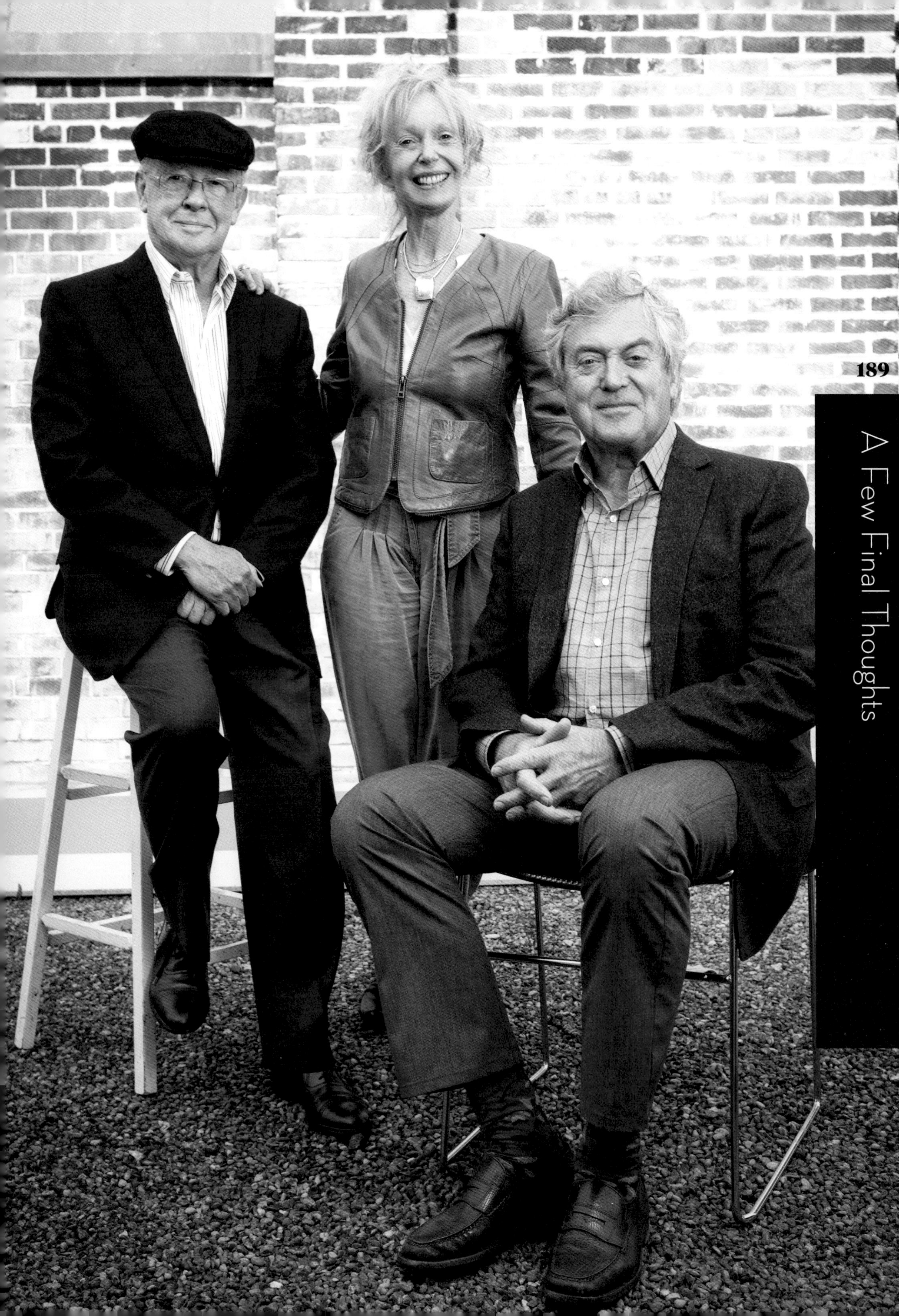

George Butterfield

When Sidney, Martha, and I started B&R fifty years ago, in 1966, we figured that the growth and survival of the company would be limited. We'd never be able to find enough young men and women to become the kind of leaders we knew we had to have. Fortunately, we were wrong. Over the years, hundreds of incredible guides have come and gone. B&R is, and has always been, rich in talented people.

In the book, there's a photo of Martha and me in Rajasthan, India. We're on top of a high white wall, with Butterfield & Robinson printed in black lettering in English and in Hindi below us. The guides had arranged to have the B&R logo painted on the wall for our group, but, as with so many things Indian, what had been planned weeks in advance happened moments before the deadline. We arrived just in time to see the painter scurrying around the back of the wall with paint can and brush in hand. As we climbed the wall moments before the photo was taken, we were careful not to smear the dripping wet paint.

The man behind the India wall painting is the man who wrote this book, Charlie Scott – guide extraordinaire. In singling out Charlie and all the other guides for special gratitude, I am not forgetting that, without the amazing team of bike mechanics, trip planners, accountants, travel advisers, and support staff who operate stealthily behind the scenes, day after day, there would be no B&R.

And to the designer of this book, Frank Viva, friend, well-known author of children's books, *New Yorker* magazine cover artist, and a major contributor to B&R's brochures for a decade or more, we owe enormous gratitude. This book was Frank's idea. No words can express our thanks to him for putting this beautifully designed and skilfully written history in our hands.

We are mindful that many people who have been part of B&R, including many past staff and our 100,000 or so loyal travellers, will have been left out of this rendition of the story. And for sure, we will have inadvertently omitted some names for our Alpha Guide list. Please know how much all of you mean to us. No history can ever record the past as it actually was, but it was something resembling Charlie's story, and it was certainly in the spirit of these pages.

At this stage in the lives of we three founders, and of B&R, it feels that it is time to pass the torch along. Our new chief, Norm Howe, formerly a B&R guide, is now clearly running the business. He is excelling – and so is B&R. Hopefully, Butterfield & Robinson will be around for years to come, and it will remain a family-controlled company. Our children, David and Nathalie, run independent businesses of their own, but both are attached to B&R, having been guides themselves. They are now involved with ownership, direction, and other B&R responsibilities.

I am not walking or biking away, but the realities of time are happening, and recently I was referred to as B&R's Spiritual Leader. Well, that's absolutely okay with me. For the foreseeable future, it gives me space to do lots of things, make many contributions, and be very busy – just the way I love to live.

Martha Robinson Butterfield

Creating this book with Charlie Scott and Frank Viva has been thrilling. Most thrilling of all has been the retrieval of fifty years of utter excitement, diversity, global exploration, and forgotten delights. George and I, Sidney, and many others have scoured our memorabilia, our old files, and the deep recesses of our minds to make it happen.

In 1966, a full half-century ago, there were no credit cards, no portable phones, no fax machines, no computers, no email. You could wire money to a European bank but, three days later, you had to spend a full day retrieving it! And then there were all the different currencies. To get the equivalent of $5 lunch money for each student every day of the trip amounted to a staggering amount of small change in Italian lira, French or Swiss francs, German marks, and British sterling. It was also cheaper then to take a ten-day cruise on the *Leonardo da Vinci* from New York to Naples, with several exotic stops along the way, than to fly from New York City to Rome.

Something in the crazy uniqueness and freedom of that first trip hooked us. There we were, two young lawyers and one art historian/archaeologist who turned our backs on our education and parental expectations to embrace the mysteries of the globe and the pleasure of bringing joy to all those who joined us. Over the years we have never wavered from our commitment to excellence, our enthusiasm for delivering the perfect trip for every traveller. The pleasure of doing that is what feeds us and sustains us.

As we look back, we are dumbfounded by the changes we have lived through. All, more or less, have been smoothly weathered with the exceptional support of thousands of game, curious, and energetic travellers and hundreds of peerless, utterly peerless, guides and staff. We celebrate you all.

It's been a great ride.

And it continues to be a great ride.

Sidney Robinson

Reconstructing more than fifty years is a daunting endeavour. Faded moments come sharply back to life, details wear the warp of time, and nostalgia throws a warm light on everything. Notwithstanding the fallibility of memory, this book somehow captures the essence of what B&R is and how it came to be.

In this dot-com world where huge global companies can appear in a few years, B&R exemplifies another approach to success. "Slow Down to See the World" is not just a marketing slogan but an approach to life. George, Martha, and I adopted this philosophy in founding B&R, but the growth of the business has been due to the travellers, the guides, and all the other people involved with us over the years who have also adopted it.

Each time a traveller reports on a what a great experience a trip has provided, I am reminded of how much B&R brings to the travel world. At a recent reception in New York City, a woman told me that since her husband died, she has travelled with B&R twelve times and that these trips have contributed enormously to her enjoyment of life. A business colleague told me that he and his wife had just returned from a walking trip in Italy and that it was as spectacular as all the other B&R trips they have enjoyed.

I am very proud of my association with B&R. It has kept me connected to my sister and brother-in-law, who have always been among my closest friends, and working with them on this book has deepened and strengthened this bond. It has also kept me connected to the magic that comes from exploring by foot and by bicycle. To this day, one of my greatest pleasures is slowing down to see the world with my wife, Linda, and my son, Luc, on B&R trips.

Notes from the Author & Designer

Butterfield & Robinson ruined me in the most wonderful way. When I graduated from university with a degree in drama, I figured I'd pursue a career in finance and resolved to be a millionaire by twenty-five. And then a friend who had led trips for B&R said, "Hey, why don't you guide bike trips in France for a summer?" Hmm, I thought, why don't I do that, happily icing my plans for a while. In the fall of 1994 I guided three trips in France. It was ridiculously fun. The following spring I returned to guide more trips in Europe, then spent a year in Morocco as B&R's "Man in Marrakech." One opportunity led to another and, over the next decade, I bounced around the world working with B&R as a guide, researcher, photographer, trip planner, and in all sorts of roles in between.

Eventually, I left to start my own business. But my heart has never strayed far from B&R. What I've learned from George, Martha, and Sidney has given my life a remarkable richness – an appreciation for people and places, art and culture, food and wine that perhaps was always there but has certainly blossomed thanks to their influence.

Working on this book has been a daunting yet hugely enjoyable honour. There were thousands of archived photos and papers to sift through, hundreds of conversations to have, and dozens of stories to discover. It is mindboggling to slow down sufficiently to realize how much ground B&R has covered over the last fifty years. And it's endlessly exciting to be reminded that curiosity, creativity, and enthusiasm are all you need to blaze a trail.

Charlie Scott

It's impossible to know or to measure how big a force George and Martha have been in my life. Back in 1995, when I first started designing catalogues for Butterfield & Robinson, I knew very little about the world. Looking back two decades later, I'm amazed that I can express an opinion about certain regional wines or a great place to eat in Verona. I have walked the Amalfi Coast, biked through vineyards in Burgundy, had a dip in a pool overlooking Positano, and dined in the former palace of a sultan in Rajasthan – all through the generosity of George and Martha. Still, it's the unexpected encounters that have left the biggest impressions, such as spending an afternoon on the beach in Normandy with a veteran on the fiftieth anniversary of D-Day. That's the true genius of Butterfield & Robinson – putting you in the right place at the right time with the right people and letting those chance encounters happen.

I was proudest of George when he agreed to spearhead the capital fundraising drive for the Sharp Centre for Design at OCAD University, my alma mater. This support for the efficacy of good design by one of Toronto's business leaders not only helped to validate the work many of my colleagues and I were doing but also provided Toronto with an internationally acclaimed landmark building. Martha has always been a hero too – her knowledge of architecture and design and her concern for the environment continue to inspire and to initiate many great conversations.

Three words come to mind when I think about George and Martha: grace, generosity, and vitality. I have received much more than I have given in this decades-long personal and professional relationship. And now to add a fourth word to the mix – gratitude.

Frank Viva

Credits

Design

Stuart Brown, Brett Ramsay, Todd Temporale, Frank Viva

Photography & Illustration

Tom Abraham, Art Gallery of Ontario, Ballard and Jarrett, David Bartholomew, Steven Bradley, Steve Brand, Stuart Brown, George Butterfield, Martha Butterfield, Aldo Cipriani, John Cullen, Brian Doben, Karen Dockrill, Juan Gali, Regina Garcia, Dick Gibb, Phil Haemmerle, Patrick Harbron, Rob Howard, Norman Howe, Jen Judge, John Lammers, Anita Kunz, Doug Laxdal, Marie Macfarlane, Stan Macfarlane, Christopher Michel, Paul Orenstein, Hill Peppard, Tim Richardson, Sidney Robinson, Deborah Samuel, Charlie Scott, Dale Sherrow, David Swales, Susan Tolnai, Frank Viva, Chris Wahl, Robert White, Storey Wilkins, Tracey Wood

A tremendous thank you to the following people for being so generous with their time, stories, guidance, and patience. Without their input and support, this book would have been four pages long and nowhere near as much fun to write.

Vicky Bake, Stephen Bayley, Erik Blachford, Jean-Louis Bottigliero, Nathalie Butterfield, David Butterfield, Martha Butterfield, George Butterfield, Stuart Brown, Peter Chittick, Paul Christopher, Benson Cowan, Brad Crockett, Jack Diamond, Tyler Dillon, Terry Dingle, M.G. Eaton, Laura Finch, Amy Fisher, Romina Fontana, Grant Gordon, Doug Grant, Cari Gray, Tom Hamilton, Kathryn Hayes, Brigitte Hogarth, Norm Howe, Trish Kaliciak, Fred Langan, Peter Langan, Juliette Lardière Butterfield, Danny Legault, Michael Liss, Marie Macfarlane, Olivier Maillard, Chris Mark, Roger Martin, Bob McDermott, Jimmy McGavin, Kelly McKinney, Richard Meech, Sally Meech, Sakis Mitsoulis, Ian Newall, John Ormond, Jim Parkinson, Hope Paterson, Robert Paterson, Massimo Prioreschi, Gil Roberts, Sidney Robinson, Nick Ross, Geoff Sandquist, John Ralston Saul, Sophia Scott, Alfie Scott, Sally Scott, Sue Scott, Rosemary Shipton, Peter Smale, Elaine Solway, Herb Solway, Nicky Speakman, Kathy Stewart, Dave Swales, Chris Tabbitt, Peter Tolnai, Nancy Towns, Dane Tredway, Muriel Truter, Frank Viva, Robin Wark, Clare Watlington, David Young, Georgia Yuill

The poem on page 188 is from the book *C. P. Cavafy: Collected Poems*. Translated by Edmund Keeley and Philip Sherrard. Edited by George Savidis (Revised edition, Princeton University Press, 1992). Reproduced with permission of Princeton University Press.

Every effort has been made to trace ownership of copyright materials. The publisher will gladly rectify any inadvertent errors or omissions in the credits of future editions.

The Butterboom (1971)

"Every time I see an adult on a bicycle, I no longer despair for the future of the human race."

H. G. WELLS